Contexts in Translating

Benjamins Translation Library

The Benjamins Translation Library aims to stimulate research and training in translation and interpreting studies. The Library provides a forum for a variety of approaches (which may sometimes be conflicting) in a socio-cultural, historical, theoretical, applied and pedagogical context. The Library includes scholarly works, reference works, post-graduate text books and readers in the English language.

Volume 41

Contexts in Translating
by Eugene A. Nida

Contexts in Translating

Eugene A. Nida

John Benjamins Publishing Company
Amsterdam/Philadelphia

™ The paper used in this publication meets the minimum requirements of American National Standard for Information Sciences – Permanence of Paper for Printed Library Materials, ANSI z39.48-1984.

Library of Congress Cataloging-in-Publication Data

Nida, Eugene Albert, 1914-
    Contexts in Translating / Eugene A. Nida.
        p.   cm. (Benjamins Translations Library, ISSN 0929–7316 ; v. 41)
    Includes bibliographical references and index.
        1. Translating and interpreting. 2. Context (Linguistics) I. Title. II. Series.

P306.2.N5   2001
418'.02--dc21   2001043494
ISBN 90 272 1647 9 (Eur.) / 1 58811 113 X (US) (Hb; alk. paper)

John Benjamins Publishing Co. · P.O. Box 36224 · 1020 ME Amsterdam · The Netherlands
John Benjamins North America · P.O. Box 27519 · Philadelphia PA 19118-0519 · USA

To my wife,
María Elena Fernández-Miranda,
my love and inspiration

Table of contents

Preface

For a number of years I have been increasingly interested in the role of contexts in understanding and translating texts, because failure to consider the contexts of a text is largely responsible for the most serious mistakes in comprehending and reproducing the meaning of a discourse. But contexts need to be understood as influencing all structural levels of a text: phonological, lexical, grammatical, and historical, including events leading up to the production of a text, the ways in which a text has been interpreted in the past, and the evident concerns of those requesting and paying for a translation.

In order to indicate precisely the implications of the roles of contexts, I have incorporated translations into English from French, Spanish, and German. And as a way of describing some of the more significant, but less known, treatments of translation, I have summarized several of these in Chapter 6 and have added Chapter 7 in order to present the three major types of theories of translation in terms of philological, sociolinguistic, and sociosemiotic principles.

I also wish to acknowledge the help that I have received from those who have reviewed certain portions of the text or who have provided help in recording questions and discussions about *Contexts in Translation* during a series of presentations of these concepts in ten universities in China during the Spring of 1999: Mona Baker, Gavin Drew, Jiang Li, Johannes P. Louw, Heping Shi, Huang Ren, Tan Zaixi, and Zhang Jing-hao.

CHAPTER 1

What is translating?

Is translating simply the act of transferring the meaning of a text from one language into another or does it depend on some theory of similarities and contrasts between languages? In order to analyze and to direct such an activity, a number of specialists in translating have elaborated numerous theories: linguistic, sociolinguistic, communicative, free, literal, hermeneutic, semiotic, relevant, skopos, Marxist, transformational, and even gender--to mention only a few. But what seems even more strange is that for the most part the best professional translators and interpreters have little or no use for the various theories of translation. They regard them as largely a waste of time, especially since most professional translators regularly and consistently violate so many rules laid down by theorists.

One reason for rejecting certain theories of translation is the fact that they are often too heavy in technical terminology and too light on illustrative examples of what top-flight translators actually do. One of the most important journals focusing on the translating of literary texts does not accept articles on theories of translating, while for Chinese translators Yan Fu's triple principle of translation, namely, "faithfulness, expressiveness, and elegance," fails to say what is to be done when these three ideal principles are not equally applicable. But according to Zhang Jing-hao this triple principle of translation advocated by Yan Fu and by many other Chinese theorists was not meant to be a key to translation theory or to translation practice. The three principles of faithfulness, expressiveness, and elegance should be understood not as competitive but as additive factors: first, faithful equivalence in meaning, second, expressive clarity of form, and third, attractive elegance that makes a text a pleasure to read. But unfortunately too many Chinese translation theorists and practitioners have focused primarily on elegance and quite naturally they concentrated their efforts on literary texts. Much the same development took place in the West, because many people assumed that only literary texts deserved or needed to be translated. As a result, most present-day theories of translation still focus on stylistics rather than on content.

What is even more discouraging is the fact that most students in programs of translation find that courses on theories of translation are the least helpful, especially when they are heavily front-loaded in a curriculum by those who do not realize that the processes and procedures in translating and interpreting are basically skills, and not compilations of information in content courses, such as literature, history, and philosophy. But this does not mean that a detailed and comprehensive study of what translators and interpreters actually do is irrelevant. In fact, such scientific studies of the semantic and semiotic aspects of interlingual communication are extremely important, as is the study of any and all types of human behavior. But the results of such studies need to be presented in understandable language and carefully integrated into creative practice. A clear understanding of the nature of interlingual communication should become general knowledge because so much of how we think and respond to new developments in science and politics is influenced by what is happening in the process of translating and interpreting. This is especially important for the success of the European Union in which all translations into all the languages have theoretically the same legal standing.

Too often textbooks on translation employ technical vocabulary that most students cannot readily grasp, and the assigned passages for translating are usually so short that students do not have the required contexts with which to make intelligent decisions about correspondences in meaning. Frequently, however, courses in translation actually turn out to be courses in language learning since university programs in foreign languages concentrate much more on literature than on the skills of listening, speaking, reading, and writing.

In translation programs students learn a great deal about foreign languages, but they usually do not learn how to use such languages in communication. As a result they waste a good deal of time in courses that are poorly organized for both language learning and for translating. In fact, relatively few students entering programs in translating have the necessary language competence to begin translating. This is not the students' fault, but the fault of the educational system.

For professional translators what counts is the effective transfer of the meaning because that is precisely what clients want and need. Their concern is not the formal features but the content of the text. For example, in documents from Spanish-speaking Latin America coming to the European Union the customary phrase *cooperación económica* is not rendered by Commission translators as "economic cooperation" but as "help" or "assistance," because that is precisely what is involved. Nevertheless, people preparing texts for the European Union continue to use *cooperación económica*, because asking directly for economic help or support would imply that these countries are economically or politically inadequate, which of course they are, or they would not be asking for financial help.

Accuracy of content should not be judged primarily in terms of "being true" to the author, but in not causing misunderstanding of the message by those for whom the translation is intended. As Jumpelt used to say about his principle of translating for the aviation industry, "I want to make sure that no one will misunderstand my translation." What clients need and generally demand is first and foremost accuracy. If a translated text can also be easy to read, this is indeed a plus factor, and if it can be culturally appropriate, the translation is obviously a success.

If completely bilingual persons have a clear understanding of a text to be translated from a source to a receptor (or target) language, they do not need to instruct their brains about how to use a noun, verb, adjective, or participle to represent a particular concept or to place a qualifying clause at the beginning or the end of a sentence, all such decisions are largely automatic because our brains are excellently organized to carry out all such decisions in a largely unconscious manner. The process of going from conceptual clarity to a verbal text is almost automatic and should be regarded as essentially no different from writing in one's own mother tongue. Clarity in understanding the source text is the key to successful translating into a receptor language. Translators do not translate languages but texts.

When, however, a text written in one's own mother tongue must be translated into a foreign language, the focus of attention shifts radically. The translator of such a text should have no difficulty understanding the text, unless it is badly written, but almost inevitably the focus of attention shifts to the linguistic features of the translation, including the proper arrangement of words, sensitivity to the style, and the relevance of the translation for receptors.

Failure to understand clearly a source text often shows up in the puzzled attempts of readers to make sense of a translation, particularly if the content is related to some new technical discipline, for example, electronics and atomic power. A similar mastery of terminology is required for translating texts involving multinational contracts. Professional translators need not only an excellent general vocabulary but also a mastery of technical terminology in two or three expanding areas of international communication, for example, merchandising, computer technology, and environmental issues.

Some source-language texts inevitably leave their mark on a translation. This is particularly true of legal texts in which there is a tradition of including within a sentence far more than is done in ordinary speech so as to have all the conditioning factors concisely combined. This is also true of many religious texts in which the verbal utterances are often regarded as sacred and divinely inspired, and therefore they must be preserved as sentence units.

Brilliant translators are, however, often surprised by the highly creative solutions that seem to pop into their heads. Such creative translators are the best examples of the fact that interlingual communication is essentially a special skill that does not necessarily depend on long years of training, although it can often be greatly enriched by studying how other translators have solved typical problems.   In many respects creative translating is like portrait painting and artistic musical performance.

On one occasion I was chatting with a man seated next to me on a flight up the Atlantic coast of the United States. He was rather embarrassed to admit that he was a portrait painter after having been a successful stock broker on Wall Street for a number of years. I immediately inquired as to where he had studied oil painting, and he admitted that he had never studied art. But when I further inquired about his background, he explained that during a period when his wife was dying of cancer, he had to be with her constantly. But he felt that he had to do something during those long tragic hours. And so he decided to buy some oil paints and paint his wife's picture.

After her death a friend was so impressed by the portrait that he asked to have his own wife's picture painted. And so began a new career in which my friend painted ten or a dozen portraits a year, but he said he was not interested in painting faces but in portraying people. Therefore he would spend a week or two living nearby and getting acquainted with the person to be painted. For his efforts he received some ten to fifteen thousand dollars for each portrait, but only if people were completely satisfied.

Some outstanding musicians know nothing about the science of harmonics, but they know how to play a piano with incredible skill, and new songs and sonatas seem to pour out of them, as though they had been stored for years in some deep recesses of the mind and were finally escaping.

Our ignorance of the ways in which our minds operate is impressive. Even in the simple activity of speaking we find it almost impossible to believe that a series of purely physical impulses, first, the air waves striking the ear drum, then, the oscillations of the tiny bones of the ear, the physical waves passing through the liquid of the ear and vibrating the cilia — all of which is purely physical — can become electro-chemical in the nerves leading ultimately to the conceptual area of the brain. How these electro-chemical physical features can be transformed into concepts — possibly by means of neural templates composed of complex patterns of synapses — is one of the two great mysteries of life — the other, being the rapidly expanding universe in which we live.

Perhaps even more mysterious is the way in which our concepts are ultimately dependent upon the clusters of sensory impressions or images of sight, taste, feeling, smell, and touch that come to us from outside of our bodies. These combine with certain internal feelings of physical well being and self awareness to make us what we are. Fortunately, we possess ways of symbolizing and understanding our experience by means of verbal sounds, and in this way we can try to make sense of our experiences. A word such as *love* may represent a number of images, and even clusters of images, suggesting such experiences as beautiful appearance, body fragrance, warmth, closeness, sexual attraction, and trust.

As Jakobson (1970, 1972) has pointed out, sociosemiotics, the science of signs in human society, tells us a great deal about the relation of signs to meaning. The iconic signs bear a formal resemblance between the verbal or visual symbol and the meaning, for example, the onomatopoeic words such as *bow-wow, cockadoodledoo, stutter* and such metaphorical expressions as *my father was a tower of strength* and *history is looking back in order to look ahead.* Imitative magic is also based on similarities, for example, making an image of a person that a voodoo priest wishes to destroy and then burning the image as curses are muttered.

On the other hand, deictic or indexical signs depend on some type of connection or association, for example, the distinction *here, there,* based on a spatial relation to some object. A metonym is often based on a part-whole relation, for example, *all hands on deck!,* a command for all sailors to be at their proper places. Associative magic also involves deictic relations, for example, the use of a lock of hair or even some uneaten food which can be used to cast a fatal spell on a hated victim. Most linguistic signs are, however, conventional, and they need to be if language is to be applicable to the endless sets of entities, activities, states, processes, characteristics, and relations existing in all the relevant aspects of human existence.

An increasing number of disciplines are also concerned with meaning, for example, communication theory, information theory, sociology, semiotics, psychology, philology, linguistics, sociolinguistics, hermeneutics, and aesthetics. Some literary critics, however, regard any published text as "public property" and no longer a part of a particular communication event. Therefore such texts are said to be open to almost any interpretation that any analyst wishes to attribute to it. But semioticians such as Jakobson, Eco, and Sebeok regard any text as a part of a communication process. And accordingly, all translating or interpreting must involve some relevant relation between the text in the source language and the text in the receptor language. At the same time, it should be clear that although this relation is never exact, there should be sufficient similarity that it can be described as having some significant measure of equivalence, described either as "the closest natural equivalent," or "as sufficiently similar that no reader of a translated text is likely to misunderstand the corresponding meaning of the source text."

1.1 A new focus on translation studies

In view of the unsatisfactory nature of many translation programs and the failure of many translation theories to provide the kind of help that professional translators can appreciate and that students can creatively employ, more and more persons concerned with translating and interpreting are turning to translation studies to form the empirical basis for a more creative approach to translating and interpreting.

A recent article in an Air France publication offered to travelers contains a fascinating interview in French with an English translation about Steven Spielberg, the famous motion-picture director. The French text uses the term *noirs* (literally, "blacks") to refer to the extras in the filming of Amistad, a film about slavery in America, but the translator wisely rendered this term as *African-Americans*, and in this way avoided a literal rendering with its negative overtones.

Similarly, the text speaks of Spielberg's astonishing success in one film after another as *Incontestablement, Spielberg a la baraka*, translated as "Spielberg is undeniably on a roll," which represents correctly the meaning of the Semitic expression *baraka* (literally, "blessed"). Furthermore, *on a roll* fits the motion-picture industry very effectively, since it is precisely the command that is often used to start the cameras functioning.

Although the French text has *La MGM, Paramount ou Warner existent depuis trois quarts de siècle*, the English translation has *MGM, Warner Bros. and Paramount have been churning out movies for more than three-quarters of a century*. In this interesting correction of the French text the translator shows clearly his greater knowledge of the American cinema industry and his close attention to detail. First, he introduces the correct designation of *Warner Bros*, and places it in the second position in line with the historical development of these producers. He also correctly renders the French *ou* as *and* (rather than *or*) and changes a generic *existent* to a critical judgment *have been churning out*, a judgment that is in line with other direct and indirect criticisms of the major producers.

The fact that not all language-cultures use similar terms for corresponding positions of responsibility creates special problems for translators. For example, the Spanish term *Presidente* refers to the president of the ruling party in Spain, whose powers are correspondingly much fewer than those of the President of the United States. Actually, the *Presidente de España* functions more as a prime minister, but this is not his title. Accordingly, translations from Spanish into English may need a footnote to explain a curious difference in the use of cognate terms.

Similarly, there were numerous misunderstandings about the role of Mao Tse-tung, who was always addressed simply as "Chairman Mao," but he had far more political and economic power than any other head of state.

1.2 Evaluation of potential translators

There is a tendency to accept academic training as a criterion of expertness in translating, since people think of translators as language professionals, and professionalism is usually judged in terms of years of study. For the translation of a technical volume from French into English about textual problems in the Hebrew Bible, the most promising translator appeared to be a complete French-English bilingual who was an editor of a journal dealing with similar subject matter. But the results were a $16,000 mistake because the translator, as well as a close colleague, simply did not understand the nature of translating. The translator matched the words but not the meaning.

On the other hand, one of the most creative translators I have ever known is Herman Aschmann, a person of limited academic training, but one who became entranced by the cultural content and literary potential of Totonaco, an Indian language of Mexico. Instead of submitting one possible rendering of a biblical expression, he usually had half a dozen different ways of representing the meaning of the Greek text. Not only did he produce an exceptional New Testament in Totonaco, but inspired local people to imitate his skill in discovering more and more meaningful ways of communicating a message into an entirely different language-culture.

Top-notch translators need to have a significant aptitude for interlingual communication, but they also need to be well grounded in the principles of transferring the meaning of a source text into a receptor language. This grounding can best be attained by experience in actual translating under the guidance of expert teachers who can present the principles of translation in terms of their own expert experience. Unfortunately, however, most institutes of translating cannot afford to pay what good translators can make in translating. And as a result, people with inferior training and experience end up teaching what they themselves have difficulty in doing.

If an agency that serves as a link between translators and clients wants to evaluate a translator's ability, it is wise to find out how three or more different translators would render a particular difficult text. Then the translated results should be judged by three or more professional translators. This may seem like an expensive procedure, but it is a far more successful assessment than accepting purely personal judgments that often fail to reveal the real underlying problems. For example, one reviewer working in a translation agency involved in evaluating translations into Chinese did not let his employer know that he was a speaker of Cantonese rather than Mandarin, and as a result his severe criticisms of translations by Mandarin speakers were seriously faulted. Similarly, an agency should not hire a Portuguese speaker to evaluate translations into Spanish, or even an American to evaluate a translation into British English.

I have lectured on theories of translation in dozens of schools and institutes, but frankly I have not been satisfied with the results, despite the numerous practical examples of interlingual equivalence. For one thing, most people have great difficulties in applying general principles to particular problems. As a result, I have found that so much more can be accomplished by sitting down with translators and helping them spot problems and test various solutions.

Many texts submitted for translation are extremely difficult to understand, although not necessarily as the result of technical terminology or figurative meanings. They are difficult to comprehend because they are so badly written. Frequently there are no indications as to the sequences of events or of ideas, and often there are predicate expressions without subjects. Such texts are many times the result of committee consultations with everyone wanting to insert some of their own ideas and with no one having the responsibility of putting a fragmented text into proper order. Learning to make sense out of nonsense is a huge and seemingly unending task for translators who must deal with the average political, financial, or technical document. And even when translators are able to telephone the writers of a text about problems of comprehension, the translators are often told that they do not need to understand the text; rather, they must simply translate it.

In fact, translators often need instruction and practice in rewriting bad texts into a more understandable form, a type of intralingual translating.

Instruction in translating between two forms or levels of the same language should be a regular part of a course in translating. For example, the following sentence occurs in a document on translation theory, "The intercultural relationship of translational issues are translated the way in which we view the translation process." Before trying to translate this English statement directly into another language, which still would not mean anything, it would be much better to translate it into intelligible English.

Such intralingual translating also has a supplementary advantage in learning how to edit a text so as to make the meaningful relations between words and phrases as clear as possible. But most textbooks on translating avoid most of these common translational problems by introducing only well written texts.

In Chinese many of the difficult poetic texts are being translated into a more modern form of language, even as Beowulf and the tales of Chaucer have been transformed into modern English.

1.3 Translating versus interpreting

Some problems arise because people think of translating and interpreting as being two entirely different kinds of operations, one written and the other spoken. But both are part of the same act of producing in a receptor language the closest natural equivalent of the source text, whether spoken or written. The significant differences are the speed with which an interpreter must make decisions, the enormous tension to keep up with the rapid flow of spoken language, the background knowledge necessary for instant recall, and the willingness to produce something that may not be "perfect." In fact, no interpretation is ever perfect.

Interpreting can, however, be an important plus for a translator, because it immediately forces him or her to be up to date with respect to rapid developments within any discipline, and it highlights the fact that listening to one language and speaking in another is a largely automatic process, something that some translators have failed to recognize.

At the former Maurice Thorez Institute of foreign languages in Moscow, persons who had already demonstrated exceptional ability as translators could also be tested for their possible ability to act as professional interpreters. The test consisted of an assigned topic, one minute to prepare, and one minute to speak. The reason for this type of testing was the conviction that interpreting, whether consecutive or simultaneous, depended more on an ability to organize information than on determining meaning.

1.4 Translating and related studies

Many people assume that translating requires considerable training in linguistics. But this is not true. Some of the best translators have no training whatsoever in linguistics, although some introduction to linguistics can make translating a much more meaningful activity. The essential skill of translators is being able to understand correctly the meaning of a source text. Knowledge of linguistics is, of course, not a handicap, but a distinct asset in clearly distinguishing between the structures of a text and the understanding of a text. Linguists analyze texts, but translators must understand texts.

Translators need to know the meanings of words in particular texts, but not necessarily all the meanings that are listed in comprehensive dictionaries. Similarly, translators do not need to analyze all the layers of grammatical structures if they can comprehend accurately the ways in which they relate to one another. The comprehension of a text as a whole is much more important to a translator than outlining the structural levels, although in some cases identification of the literary structures can provide insight for the correct understanding of a text.

Serious attention may also be required for evaluating the capacity of students to use foreign languages, because most students entering programs of translation are usually not adequately prepared to translate, and as a result they often acquire habits that are not easy to break. The real issue is the best use of students' time and energy in learning a foreign language in the most efficient manner. Great advances have been made in the field of language learning, and programs in language learning should be designed to take advantage of such insights and methods.

At some point in all programs of language learning some experience in translating should be introduced, but not on the elementary level of simply trying to make sense, but at more advanced levels in which translating can test the adequacy of vocabulary for certain types of texts. The translation of various types of texts is particularly useful in highlighting the differences of style in different types of discourse.

Some programs in translation also try to provide students with extensive information about such supplementary fields as computational linguistics and artificial intelligence, but such information is only marginal to the practical concerns of most translators and interpreters. Far more important is the need to appreciate fully the importance of the intended audience. In fact, no translator should begin to work without first knowing who is the intended audience, as determined by the publisher. For example, is the publication for children, middle-school pupils, university level students, professionals, adults who are retooling for new or expanded careers, or golden-age retirees?

Translators also need to know if a translation would become more relevant if the features of format (paragraphing, indentation, shifts in style, type face, spacing, and bullets) were adjusted to the meaningful elements in the text. In addition, the existence of previously published translations of a text inevitably conditions people's thinking about a revision or a new translation of such texts as the Bible, Shakespeare's dramas, and the Greek and Latin Classics. During the process of translating a series of tests of the translation with representative groups of the presumed audience can always be helpful.

1.5   The contents and structure of this volume

No book can possibly cover all the elements that influence the work of a translator or interpreter, but this volume at least tries to deal in a systematic way with some of the principal issues. The following chapters attempt to answer the question posed by this chapter, namely, "What is translating?" Accordingly, Chapter 2 is concerned with the relation between language and culture, because a language is always a part of a culture and the meaning of any text refers directly or indirectly to the corresponding culture. Chapter 3 then takes up the issue of translating words in context since the choice of particular words and their meanings depend primarily on various aspects of the context: other nearby words, the subject matter, the presumed audience, and especially the meanings of those words that so often do not mean what they say, for example, figurative expressions, indirect responses, and proverbs.

Chapter 4 focuses on the grammatical connections between words, and Chapter 5 is concerned with the structures and style of discourse and how these influence the translation of a text on all levels. Chapter 6 includes a number of representative treatments of translation, and Chapter 7 discusses three major types of translation theories.

CHAPTER 2

Language and culture

Language is a set of verbal symbols that are primarily auditory, but secondarily written, now in more than 2,200 different languages with more than 400 orthographic systems for computer adaptation. Language also constitutes the most distinctive feature of a culture, which may be described in a simplistic manner as the totality of the beliefs and practices of a society. And although a language may be regarded as a relatively small part of a culture, it is indispensable for both the functioning and the perpetuation of the culture. Accordingly, competent translators are always aware that ultimately words only have meaning in terms of the corresponding culture. But while a language can usually be acquired within a period of ten years, it takes a lifetime to understand and become an integral part of a culture.

In order to understand and appreciate the related roles of language and culture as two interdependent symbolic systems, it may be helpful to describe some of their more relevant similarities, differences, and interrelations. Their similarities can perhaps be best understood in terms of early acquisition, loss, collective activity, variability, change, bundles of features, and sociosemiotic factors. The differences can also be described in terms of language as the most distinctive feature of a culture, a code that can speak about itself, linear arrangement, entities that have no measurable existence, and the underlying forces that sustain and drive the culture. The interrelations between language and culture can then be described in terms of reciprocal modifications, the rates of change, the representation of culture by language, and the issues of double causation.

An utterance normally means something, but speeches by politicians often say nothing, and that is precisely why a group of translators at the United Nations unanimously agreed that the most difficult texts to translate or interpret are those that contain no meaning. A translator or interpreter normally searches for meaning because that is precisely the function of a discourse, but there are speakers who have nothing to say or prefer to speak without saying anything — a skill that some politicians seem to possess to a point of perfection.

Cultural practices may also be regarded as having meaningful purposes.

When a person buys a large home in an exclusive neighborhood, there may be several alternative or overlapping meanings: a place to house a large family, a way of showing off one's wealth, a place for entertaining large numbers of guests, and a good investment. Knowing the appropriate meaning of a nonlinguistic event also depends on the context of who does what, when, where, and for what reason, just as the meaning of the word *run* depends largely on contexts: *the dogs were running, the salmon are running, he is running into debt, his nose is running*. In fact, the term *run* combines with a number of diverse contexts to provide distinct concepts.

2.1 Similarities between language and culture

2.1.1 Language and culture acquisition

Both language and culture are acquired at a very early age and in the largely unstructured contexts of home and playground. Furthermore, both language and culture seem to be frozen by upper adolescence, after which time most people find it very difficult to learn a foreign language without a noticeable accent. They also feel "more at home" in the culture of their upper adolescence, when most of the automatic patterns of behavior are seemingly accepted as the most appropriate.

Children acquire a language at a much earlier age than most people imagine. In one case an American family working for many years in Thailand needed to return to the United States for another assignment, but nine months before their return they had a baby girl. The parents were, however, so occupied with winding up numerous responsibilities that they were forced to leave the baby girl with a Thai maid most of the time.

When the baby was nine months of age, the family returned to the United States and three months later the baby began to speak, but she spoke Thai, not English. During the months with the Thai maid the baby had learned the right tonal patterns, a vocabulary that fit her needs, and an arrangement of words that showed a remarkable instinct for the grammar of Thai.

It is also interesting that children who have grown up speaking a local language may seem to have completely forgotten it after a few years in a completely different language-culture. But a return to the local area somehow prompts an amazing recall of the language. One member of a team of linguists going to Mexico had lived in Spanish-speaking Latin America until the age of twelve, but seemingly had completely forgotten Spanish. But within three months of being in Mexico his Spanish came bouncing back, and he was accused of having deceived his colleagues about not knowing Spanish. Apparently, the mind never forgets anything completely.

The skillful learning of a culture may also occur at a very early age. Most children by two years of age know exactly how to pit their parents against each another in order to get what the children want. They quickly learn the pecking order of their culture, and they know whom they can hit without being hit back.

2.1.2 The loss of a language and culture

By not participating fully in a language-culture, people may also lose linguistic skills. Many teen-age Navajos in large centers are gradually losing their facility to speak Navajo, although they may still be able to understand what older people say. When being interviewed on radio, they often express their regret in not being able to speak, and they usually blame their university studies for making them linguistically deficient in their mother tongue.

In some instances the loss of language proficiency may involve only one aspect of a mother-tongue competence. For example, in most Protestant Spanish-speaking churches in New Mexico, the entire service is in Spanish, except for the reading of the Bible, which is usually done by laymen in English. The reason for this partial deficiency in one's mother tongue is due to the fact that Spanish is the medium of oral communication, while English is the primary language of written communication: newspapers, magazines, signs, and advertisements.

Young people who pass upper adolescence in a foreign language-culture often prefer to stay abroad. And even after advanced education in the language-culture of their parents, they frequently prefer an overseas job because they seem to feel more at home. This is precisely why American parents on overseas assignment are often urged by their companies to have their children return to the "home country" as soon as they complete their basic six or eight years of education.

2.1.3 Language and culture as collective activities

Both language and culture are collective enterprises, and no one person ever controls completely a language or a culture. Furthermore, only a relatively large group of people can transport a language or a culture from one place to another. For example, a number of Indians along the Caribbean coast of Honduras speak the Miskito language and live their lives like most other

Indians along the coast, but in appearance many more closely resemble the people of West Africa. This strange lack of agreement between language-culture and physical features can be explained by the fact that the West African features are due to the fact that most slaves who escaped from the islands of the Caribbean came one or two at a time in small canoes, entirely too few people to carry with them their language or their culture. Accordingly, they intermarried with the local people and adopted their language and culture. In order to retain a language and culture there must be a critical number of interacting people to form and maintain a language-culture.

Even a shaman's chanting to heal a sick person usually depends on the presence of an extended family, who must confess their violations of tribal rules or their hidden jealousies in order to prepare the way for an act of healing. Language and culture are essentially collective enterprises, whether in talking about building boats with irregularly cut pieces of bread-fruit trees in mid-Pacific islands or in navigating across hundreds of miles of the Pacific Ocean in outrigger canoes.

When indigenous people are first exposed to the outside world and to the diseases for which they have no natural immunity, as many as one half to two thirds of the people may die before they acquire a degree of immunity or resistance. For example, the Paacas Novas people of eastern Peru and Western Brazil died off from a population of 300 to approximately 100 before the remaining fragments of the tribe decided to return to the jungle. The history of the native people of Hawaii is similar, but there was no place to which they could escape.

2.1.4 Variability

Variability is the name of the game for both language and culture. In fact, the voice print of each person is completely distinctive, and persons concerned with identification of people insist that the voice print is even more distinctive than finger prints. Furthermore, two pronunciations of the same phrase by the same person are always somewhat different, in the same way that no two performances of the same dance are ever identical. And an expert cook never twice prepares the same dish in exactly the same way. This makes home-cooking so much less monotonous than restaurant fare.

One effective way to test variability in language is to employ a game involving twelve or more people who are asked to whisper in order a complex sentence of twenty words to the next person in line. An original sentence such as "When they had all arrived, the chairman told them to forget about court procedures but to take an immediate straw vote on guilt or innocence" will probably end up as something like "When the chairman got there, the jury decided that the criminal was guilty."

Groups of people also adopt special ways of speaking, for example, the medical and legal professions, as well as the Mafia of Europe and America and the Triads of Asia. Geographical dialects of a language are typical of what takes place when a language is spoken over an extended area for several centuries, for example, the series Dutch, Low German, High German, and Switzer Dietsch (the German dialect in Switzerland).

People speaking contiguous dialects can usually understand one another, but not the people who are two or more dialects from one another. Within England itself there are dialects of English that are much more diverse than the more or less standard forms of Hong Kong English, New Zealand English, Australian English, Philippines English, Indian English, South African English, British English, and American English. Rather than such different forms of English becoming more and more alike, they are actually becoming more and more distinctive.

What is true of geographical dialects is equally true of sociolinguistic dialects. Received English, the language of the exclusive secondary schools of England, is being threatened by some people in the computer industry who imitate American usage, and there are always those few snobs who want to put on airs by using outlandishly "exalted" language. To my remark about an "unexpected rain" the night before in Southern California, my neighbor replied, "Oh yes, a little unpremeditated precipitation."

Different interpersonal contexts result in quite different forms of language. These registers of language are typically on five different levels: ritual (the language of ceremonies and rites), formal (language used in speaking to people one does not know), informal (conversing with business colleagues), casual (at a sports event), and intimate (language used within a family), which Joos (1972) describes so effectively in a book entitled "Five Clocks."

The culture also parallels these same five levels of language by having at least five levels of clothing: tuxedo (also called "smoking"), business suit, sports outfit, beachwear, and bathrobe. The style of language used for a particular communication also differs greatly. Churchill could have warned the world about the pain and suffering that World War II would bring by spelling out the loss of life, the sacrifices of labor, and the personal sorrow that the people would experience, but he put it all into three short words, "blood, sweat, tears."

Variability also exists in culture, perhaps nowhere better demonstrated than in the way people greet one another. In America exceptionally good friends of the opposite sex kiss once and usually near the mouth but without touching the lips, while in Spain such people kiss twice, first on the right cheek and then on the left cheek. In Belgium people normally kiss three times, right, left, and right, but in France people frequently kiss four times: right, left, right, left.

The system of traffic lights employing green, yellow, and red is quite similar in various parts of the world, but frequently there are variations. In Moscow the yellow light normally occurs before and after a red light, and in some parts of China an illuminated sign indicates the number of seconds before the traffic light will change. In Argentina, however, drivers seem to pay little or no attention to traffic lights. One Argentinean explained his lack of concern for stop lights by saying, "A red light, when there is no car in sight, is an insult to my intelligence."

At Chinese banquets in universities the honored guest is usually seated opposite to the entrance to the dining room, and other persons seat themselves according to their academic rank, but a government official, irrespective of rank, takes precedence over all but the honored guest. In fact, in China government officials have been traditionally referred to as "father and mother officials," a highly significant terminology in a Confucianist society

2.1.5 Change

Change in language is a corollary of its inherent variability. In some instances the change seems to be particularly drastic, for example, the change from Arabic to Roman orthography for writing Turkish, a clear symbol of Turkey's shift from a Middle East orientation to one facing Western Europe.

Shortly after the victory of the Communist leadership in China, many persons in positions of political responsibility urged a change in orthography from typical Chinese characters to an alphabetic system, but such a change was regarded as entirely too radical because it would cut off succeeding generations from the rich heritage of literature and calligraphic art. The leadership did, however, decide to employ simplified characters and even published a list of some 3,000 characters in which all official business should be conducted and reported.

English is one of the major world languages and also the one that has probably borrowed the most from other languages. In fact, less than half of the vocabulary is Anglo-Saxon. Changes, however, may be only partial or affect only certain aspects of a language. For example, Spanish has been very conservative in keeping to traditional distinctions in verb tenses, but very open to changes in spelling, while French has been intensively conservative in spelling but much more open to change in the use of the verb system.

These same seemingly arbitrary decisions with respect to change in language also apply to cultural features. In Great Britain shifting from pounds, shillings, and pence to a decimal system required considerable pressure over a number of years, and the complete shift in America from yards, feet, and inches to a metric system will require a number of more years. But some changes, especially in culture, may be only cosmetic. Some communists in Europe use socialist terminology as a means of hiding their ultimate purposes.

2.1.6 Bundles of linguistic and cultural features

Rarely does one particular feature of a language or culture occur alone. For languages there are almost always a bundle of features that combine to communicate a message. The most obvious of these features are the paralinguistic ones of voice quality, speed of utterance, loudness, hesitations, and stuttering — all of which carry along an additional message or impede communication. For example, excessively rapid speech may indicate that the speaker has far more to say than the time allotted, but it can also mean an attempt to hide the real content by speaking more rapidly than people can understand.

Constant interrupting of a speaker in a social setting is regarded as very bad in most of northern Europe and America, but in the Mediterranean areas it is not only an approved feature, but people defend their intrusions by saying that by interrupting they show the speaker that they are interested in what is being said.

Language and culture often combine in a kind of symbiosis. In the United States people normally stand about one arm's length apart when conversing, but in the eastern part of the Mediterranean world people are usually not more than half that distance apart. Accordingly, North Americans tend to react negatively to what seems to be aggressiveness by people in the Middle East, while local people interpret the action of North Americans as being too standoffish and unfriendly.

In some societies the amount of time that a person must wait before responding to what has been said is astonishingly long. When Tarahumara Indians in northern Mexico are discussing an important issue, turn-taking normally requires that a second speaker must not only wait for the first speaker to complete what he wishes to say, but he must continue to remain silent for at least as long as the first speaker spoke. Only then is it polite to present a different viewpoint. Time spent waiting becomes a signal to the audience that the following speaker has thoroughly considered everything said by the previous speaker, but he still disagrees. Such discussions seem interminably long to Americans, who expect a respondent to immediately jump to his feet. Furthermore, among the Tarahumara gestures are regarded as particularly offensive because they appear to represent physical threats.

Culture is also expressed by bundles of features. For example, in Brazil clothing is a major element in marking class distinctions. And in proportion to income Brazilians expend much more for attractive clothing than do North Americans. But in England some of the richest persons seem to prefer their old rumpled clothing as an inverted symbol of their status. In other words they have so much money that they do not have to dress well to symbolize their position in society.

Sometimes a cultural feature may be so overdone that people need to find a more practical solution. During banquets in China people enjoy series of toasts to almost anyone and for almost every purpose. But this usually requires everyone to stand up and reach out, even across a wide table, to clink glasses with each person. After a while this can be too much, and accordingly, more and more people are simply clinking their glasses on the revolving glass serving center.

American business letters are usually relatively short and right to the point, but a literal translation of such letters into Spanish almost always gives Latin Americans the impression that North Americans are unfriendly. On the other hand, letters coming from Latin America to North American business men are frequently so effusive with praise that the writers seem insincere. Intelligent bilingual secretaries soon resolve such problems by deleting effusive praise from letters coming from Latin America and by adding expressions that will make their American bosses appear more friendly to business men in Latin America.

2.1.7 Sociosemiotic elements in language and culture

The most obvious sociosemiotic features of language and culture are iconic (based on similarity), deictic (based on association), and conventional, without any formal connection between form and meaning.

One of the most common iconic features of language is the parallelism between temporal and narrative sequences in history, novels, biography, and even prophecy. The cultural iconic signs are even more obvious, for example, a roadside sign of a knife and fork to indicate a restaurant in Europe and America. Almost all designations for toilets include stylized pictures of a woman wearing a skirt and of a man with full length straight pants.

Typical deictic signs are usually two-dimensional in English, *here/there*, *this/that* but in Spanish there is an unusual three dimensional contrast: *aquí* "here," *allí* "there," and *allá* "there even further away." Familiar cultural signs include arrows to point the way, painted lines to mark traffic boundaries, and painted piping to show the flow of various substances in chemical plants.

Most vocabulary of any and all languages is conventional, that is, there is no one-to-one relation between the sounds and the meanings of words. Furthermore, the boundaries of meaning of practically all words in any language are fuzzy and indefinite. For example, how thick must a thread be in order for it to be called a string, or how thick does a string have to be before it is called a cord, or how thick is a cord before it is regarded as a rope. Government bureaus on weights and measures usually legislate such matters for the sake of taxes and import duties, but for the general public all such words have very indefinite boundaries of meaning.

But sets of words are not restricted to such obviously related series as *thread, string, cord, rope*, etc. There are a number of different kinds of meaningfully related sets of terms:

Clusters: *run, walk, dance, jump*
Inclusions: *walk* as including *shuffle, amble, march, parade*
Overlapping: *love/like, dine/eat, chew/masticate*
Reversives: *tie/untie, brief/debrief*
Direction of participation: *borrow/lend, buy/sell*
Positive/negative: *yes/no, affirm/deny*
Series
    Infinite: *one, two, three*, etc.
    Repetitive: *Monday, Tuesday, Wednesday*, etc.
    Graded: *private, corporal, sergeant, lieutenant, major*, etc.

Within a culture there are also important sets constituting cultural domains, for example, eating, bathing, talking. The set involving eating relates to time, place, with whom, what, how and the order in which food is served and eaten.

2.1.8 Illogical features of language and culture

For the most part the systematic relations of meaning within semantic domains seem to be quite logical. Some numerical systems are built on series of 10s, others on 20s and still others on a so-called blanket system based on the process of folding cloth, but even in the decimal systems there are a number of unsystematic sets, for example, in English the numbers *eleven* and *twelve* are not consistent with the following numbers ending in *-teen*, for example, *thirteen, fourteen*, etc. In French the number system becomes irregular at several points, for example, 70 is literally "sixty-ten" and 80 is "four-twenties."

The meaning of compound words cannot always be determined by the constituent parts, for example, in English a *set-up* and an *up-set* are distinctly different although they contain the same verbal components. It is the arrangement that counts.

The ordinal and cardinal numbers of the months do not fit in English. For example, the names of the last four months of the year, namely, *September, October, November, December* contain the Latin numbers for seven, eight, nine, and ten, but these are the ninth, tenth, eleventh, and twelfth months of the year. This anomaly occurred because Roman calendar-makers wanted the year to begin at the time of the Roman Saturnalia festival when the sun began to return north. People would rather live with an anomaly than alter the names.

There are also numerous anomalies in culture. For example, in order to take advantage of longer days during the summer, it is much easier to turn back the clock than it is to adjust to a presumably different time of day. In the Western World people pay to have their fortune told, even when most of the generalities never prove true. But in India a person can pay to have a guru tell them the nature of their earlier reincarnations. First, a person's finger print is taken and then presumably matched with an infinite number of existing finger prints and at last a scribe reads off what has been written down on seemingly endless rolls. As can be readily recognized, reading reincarnations is a much safer and easier profession than fortune-telling.

2.1.9 The location of language and culture

Many people wrongly assume that language and culture must exist in dictionaries, grammars, and encyclopedias, but this is obviously not true. Such books are only limited attempts to describe some of the more salient features of these two interrelated patterns of behavior. The real location of language and culture is in the heads of participants.

There is a wide-spread account of Bloomfield's answer to an inquiry about how long it would take him to write a complete grammar of the English language. He is claimed to have said that if he had twenty well-trained linguistic assistants and twenty years, he could probably produce a fairly accurate account of the English language. But by that time the language would no doubt have changed significantly, and according he would never be able to catch up.

When any author reviews his own early publications, he soon realizes how rapidly languages change, but also how tenacious are some of the awkward illogical forms, for example, the irregular forms of the verb *to be*: *am, is, are, was, were, been* as well as how quickly an abbreviation like *Ms*, as a compromise between *Miss* and *Mrs*, can be accepted.

2.2 Differences

2.2.1 Language as a distinctive part of culture

Although language is clearly a part of culture, it is also one of its most distinctive features. One night I was waiting for a plane in the Cairo airport, when in came a group of people speaking Japanese, but they did not behave like Japanese. There was no tourist guide carrying a little flag, and the men did not gather around a prestigious man, nor did the women gather around a prestigious woman. Furthermore, the people were noisy as they mixed freely, joked, and laughed. In addition, they did not dress like Japanese tourists.

I became so curious about these people that I finally spoke to a woman who appeared to be rather cosmopolitan in her behavior, and I asked in English, "Where do you come from?" to which she immediately replied, "Oh, we're all Americans from Hawaii." The people had retained their language, but had so radically changed their other patterns of behavior that they seemed to constitute a cultural anomaly.

2.2.2 Distinctive elements of language

Language is not only a distinctive feature of a group of people, but it is also different from other codes in that it can be used to speak about itself. This means that language can be used to describe its own structures. Written codes, whether alphabetic, syllabic, or ideographic (as in the case of Chinese), are all secondary in the sense that they are codes to represent language. The DNA, however, is also a primary code, but it is not able to be used to analyze itself.

Language is also structurally linear in that it moves in one spatial direction, although it may combine with gesture codes (movements of face, hands, head, shoulders, and stance) to reinforce and even to negate the meaning of words, as in the case of a screamed utterance of "I love you!" while twisting the face into a picture of hate.

Although language is rightfully described as structurally linear, the understanding of language does not precede in merely one direction. The real meaning of a word may depend on a context that occurs on a following page. Furthermore, fast reading of a text using a system described as "speed reading" depends on assimilating the meaning of a passage by reading successively different portions of a page containing three or four lines at a time. Moreover, in reading narrow-column texts, as in most newspapers and popular magazines, a reader does not look back and forth for each line, but simply glides rapidly down the text while concentrating on the content vocabulary and passing over many formal markers, such as prepositions and conjunctions, since the meaning of such linking words is usually predictable from the contexts. At the same time, however, close attention must be given to negatives and modals of probability, for example *may, could, possibly.*

This process of reading is essentially based on the principle of reading by contexts rather than by lines, since so frequently the meaning of words depends on what follows rather than on what precedes.

Understanding oral language precedes very much the same way. In general, a hearer does not tick off the meanings of words one at a time, but assimilates a language by chunks, as much as twelve seconds at a time. This process usually works quite well as long as a person understands clearly the topic of the discourse. Otherwise, a series of comments, without a topic to which to relate the comments, can be very frustrating.

2.2.3 The creation of cultural symbols

A culture creates and endows certain entities with important cultural significance. A path may become for some tribal people a way of explaining their traditional way of life. As long as the people can remember, each generation has walked the same path. For the Buddhist world, however, the wheel is the appropriate symbol to represent constant change that always reverts to its original position, a kind of rotational reincarnation. Other cultures live in the shadow of a golden age, which was not really so golden, but it seems to constitute a goal to recapture. But still other cultures place their trust in a messiah who will come at the critical point in history and remake the chaotic world.

Perhaps the most unusual feature of culture is its capacity to treat as real a number of entities and concepts that have no measurable existence, for example, mermaids, unicorns, demons, jinns, angels, heaven, hell, reincarnation, horoscopes, clairvoyance, fortune telling, a rabbit's foot, tea leaves, and lines in a person's hand.

A culture may actually reinterpret a symbol. Classical Greeks regarded the *daimones* as beneficent intermediaries between the gods and humans, but the Christians largely transformed such spiritual entities into fearful demons.

2.2.4 Language as a four-level system

Language consists of four distinct levels of signs: sounds, words, grammar, and discourse, with seemingly no one central cerebral region for integration or control of verbal communication. But for culture there seem to be certain drives that combine to make decisions favorable to each person: especially, self-preservation, power, and belonging. Self-preservation seems to be one of the most fundamental drives, even in circumstances in which death would seem to be much more advantageous. The concern for power, whether political, physical, or monetary, is also a vital factor in making decisions, but many people place an even higher price on the sensation of being accepted and belonging to others.

2.2.5 The use of language by culture

(1) providing information about the processes and the values of a culture (education is mastering the information regarded as essential for being a part of a society), (2) directing the activity of a culture (traditionally described as the imperative function), (3) establishing and maintaining a positive emotional state for the participants within a culture (the emotive function), (4) ritual alteration in the status of participants in a culture, for example, marriage vows, sentencing of criminals, religious ritual, internment of the dead (the performative function), (5) interpersonal relations (who speaks to whom about what and in what manner), (6) cognitive activity (the most common use of language is in thinking, although some thoughts are not necessarily expressed in words), (7) recreative (the use of language in games, for example, scrabble, crossword puzzles, word-guessing games on television, verbal challenges involving poetry and song), and (8) aesthetics, the use of language for aesthetic expression, especially in poetry and elegant prose.

2.3 Interrelations between language and culture

2.3.1 Differences in culture mean differences in language

Because Hebrew, Greek, and Latin all had three distinct terms for *body, soul, spirit*, people throughout the Middle Ages in Western Europe thought that there must be three fundamental aspects or parts of human personality. Descartes, however, insisted that in place of three features there are only two: the physical and the nonphysical, a distinction that has largely dominated popular psychology until now. But more and more neurophysiologists and psychologists find no way to separate the body and the spirit. The fact that fully 50% of diseases have certain psychosomatic factors involved has seemed further evidence that people do not consist of two parts, but only of one complex unity, as argued so effectively in the recent volume, "*Descarte's Error*" by Domasio (1994).

When a culture experiences radical change, the vocabulary also undergoes corresponding alterations. For example, the cattle-raising Anuaks of the Sudan and Ethiopia had thousands of technical terms for various colors, shapes, sizes, and ages of cattle, but at one time they had only one word for everything made of metal. But after the arrival of small steam boats on the tributaries to the Nile and after airplanes began landing on the lakes made by the meandering rivers, the Anuaks starting living and working in a different technological world. Within a few years they created thousands of new terms for parts of motor boats and airplanes, as well as for electric lights, flashlights, motors, and even computers. All of these changes have brought radical changes of wealth and power for a society that has had a long tradition of belief in "limited good," that is to say, the existence of only so much "good" in the world, and anyone who seems to have a disproportionate amount of possessions or power, must have taken some of these "goods" away from others.

In the neighboring Shilluk tribe family members destroyed a young orchard planted by a younger brother who was likely to become much richer than any other member of the family. He would then have much more spirit power than any one else, and this would destroy the family solidarity. Among the Hopi Indians of the Southwest United States something of this same attitude exists, and accordingly children hesitate to excel in school because this tends to disturb the sense of equality within a group.

2.3.2　The rate of change in language and culture

The rate of change within a language-culture depends on a number of factors. But in almost all situations the change in culture appears to be faster than change in language. This conservatism in language has an important implication for self-preservation, since the need to communicate effectively needs to be something so conservative that people will have no doubts as to the meaning of a sentence. But it does seem strange that languages also appear to change directly proportionate to the density of communication. It would seem only natural that peripheral dialects would change more rapidly than a central dialect since they would be only on the edge of a speech community. Nevertheless, it is the dense center of language use that undergoes the greatest and the most rapid change. In other words the language of Paris changes faster than the French of Guadeloupe or New Caledonia. Similarly, the English spoken from Boston to Washington DC is changing faster than the English of Memphis Tennessee or Prince Edward Island in Canada.

High-school students in Iceland can read and understand Icelandic sagas from 9th Century, while Americans have great difficulty trying to understand Chaucerian English from the 14th Century.

2.3.3　Partial representation of the culture by language

Language represents the culture because the words refer to the culture, as the beliefs and practices of a society, but the representation is never complete or perfect. Changes in language inevitably tend to lag behind changes in culture, but there are also aspects of culture that are so taken for granted that people simply do not feel the need for terminology to talk about what is completely obvious. For certain aspects of experience there may be a significant shortage of specific terms. For example, the verb *lie* refers to saying or writing something that is not true, and a person can use *prevaricate* (with the usual implication of oral language) or *falsify* (often related to documents). But what about *white lies* (those that generally do no harm to anyone, other than to the liar) and *black lies* (those that are obviously untruths and harmful). But there are also exaggerations that cross the line into lies, and there are understatements that do the same. There are also political promises that everyone, including the speaker, realizes can never prove true, and there is also slanted advertising, justified because it offers the audience "a chance to decide for themselves." Perhaps so much of modern life is a lie that we are numbed to the distinctions that constantly assail us on television, bill boards, newspapers, magazines, internet, and books.

2.3.4 Double causation

In many parts of Africa violent death is usually attributed to double causation. A man killed by lightning is first the victim of the lightning bolt, but most African medicine men will also claim that someone must have been practicing black magic so as to make sure that the man would be in precisely the place where the lightning would strike.

People who believe in horoscopes likewise believe in double causation, because good luck or tragedy must be due in part to favorable or unfavorable positions of the planets and stars at the time of a person's birth. This is simply astronomical predeterminism or predestination. Those who find solace in tea leaves or in crystals are likewise addicts of double causation. But perhaps those who attribute all good and evil fortune to saints, angels, jinns, or the spirits in the caves are similarly to be pitied.

CHAPTER 3

Words in context

Anyone attempting to understand the meaning of words in context should probably first consider some of the serious misconceptions about their meanings, especially the idea that the words of any language constitute a rich mosaic of terms that fit together neatly into various semantic domains or fields. There are no neat verbal mosaics, because the meanings of words constantly overlap with one another and the boundaries of meaning are fuzzy and poorly defined, for example, the series *love, like, adore, worship, be crazy about, be head over heals in love with.* Even in the short series of *sprint, dash, race* there is considerable overlapping in referring to the act of rapid running. *Sprint* seems to focus more on the rapid and effective movement of the legs, and *race* suggests competition, while *dash* appears to emphasize simply fast movement in space, without regard to style. The real clues to meaning depend on contexts.

In some sets of terms there may be quite evident features of degree, for example, *work, labor, toil, slave,* but the relative amount of effort involved cannot be plotted mathematically because so much depends on the particular contexts in which such words occur.

Most people assume that the meaning of nouns derived from verbs can be easily recognized because they have predictable meanings, especially when a verb occurs with the common suffix *-er.* But the word *runner* does not always refer to someone who runs. For example, *runner* may also refer to a long piece of metal on which a sled or sleigh glides, or even to the blade of ice-skates. But *runner* may also refer to a long, narrow rug used in a hall or to a slender stolon of a straw-berry bush, or even to a smuggler who must run blockades. This same suffix may also occur on stems that never occur in isolation, for example, *carpenter,* but as *-or* in *doctor* and *benefactor* as well as *-eur* in *chauffeur* (borrowed from French).

Some people believe that knowledge of the true meanings of words depends on knowing the history of their development, but etymology is often quite misleading. For example, most people assume that the component *by-* in *bylaw, byproduct, bypath* refers to some type of subordinate or derived *law, product, path.* Historically, however, the *by-* in *bylaw* is derived from *burgh,* that is, the law of a town, not of a county or province, but its meaning has been reinterpreted to refer to a law that is not a part of a constitution but is a supplementary document defining more specifically some of the provisions of a constitution.

Conversely, most people assume that *duck* in *he shot a duck* and *he tried to duck a blow* must represent an entirely different kind of word history. In reality, however, the two occurrences of *duck* are historically related and are based on the typical behavior of a water fowl that is famous for ducking under the surface of the water.

Although most people assume that languages are essentially unchangeable, the truth is that all living languages are in the constant process of change. Sometimes the change is rapid and obvious, as when the English term *gay* became primarily a designation of homosexuals. In Spanish the verb *coger*, a very common term traditionally meaning "to take," became a common expression for having sexual intercourse.

Because many languages form new words by adding words together, that is, by compounding, as in *breakwater, gaspipe, nonsense, gentleman*, some people assume that this is what always happens. But some words are the result of shortening, for example, *intercom* for *intercommunication system* and *photo* for *photograph*.

Many people also believe that dictionaries are the final authority and depository of all the words of a language. There are, however, some words that never get into a dictionary, for example, short-lived adolescent slang and rapidly evolving technical terms of science. In fact, by the time a dictionary is compiled and published it is almost always at least twenty-five years out of date, especially in the listing of idioms.

In many instances dictionaries become so succinct that they do not help a reader. For example, the relatively common term *carbohydrate* is defined as "any of a class of organic compounds that are polyhydroxy aldehydes or polyhydroxy ketones, or change to such substances on simple chemical transformations, as hydrolysis, oxidation, or reduction." If a person can understand this definition, then he certainly doesn't need to look up the word *carbohydrate*. The definition is true but almost meaningless for the majority of people who want information about the substances that make up a carbohydrate. For translators encyclopedias are often much more helpful than dictionaries.

Many people assume that lists of synonyms provide all the words that mean the same as a key term. In reality, however, there are no complete synonyms in the sense of two words having exactly the same designative (denotative) and associative (connotative) meanings. One dictionary lists as synonyms of *form* the following terms: *mold, appearance, cast, cut, figure, shape, outline,* but such terms approximate the meaning of *form* only in highly specific (texts. Other dictionaries list as synonyms of *distress* such words as *anguish*, which seems much more emotional in content, and *hardship*, which is much less acute than *distress*. Actually, the listing of synonyms and antonyms is largely misleading because the necessary contexts that would justify assembling such terms into semantic domains or fields are not given.

Because both dictionaries and grammars seem to focus on the rules and laws of a language, they suggest to many people that languages are essentially regular and competely rule governed. In fact some of the most interesting aspects of language are swept away by some linguists as mere subcategorizations. But for English even the regularities of the orthography largely mask the irregularities of the pronunciations. Past tense verb forms such as *judged, clipped, grabbed, picked* are all monosyllabic, pronounced as *jujd, clipt, grabd, pikt*, in which the final consonant is voiced or voiceless depending on the preceding consonant, but a word such as *landed* consists of two syllables in which the second syllable consists of a central vowel followed by a *d*. The doubling of the medial consonants and the regularity of the written form of words (an aspect of graphemics, rather than phonemics) is probably an advantage for the average reader of English.

In comparison with a number of other languages in the Indo-European family, English seems much more regular in its formations, but for some of its most common words the changes in tense forms are extensive, for example, *make/made, go/went, am/are/is/was/were/be/been*. Such irregularities can only be explained by the fact that these words are so common; otherwise, they would have been leveled by analogy to regular formations.

3.1 The types and functions of contexts in understanding texts

3.1.1 Syntagmatic contexts

In determining the meanings of words the role of the context is maximized and the role of any focal element is minimized, which means that the context actually provides more distinctiveness of meaning than the term being analyzed (Joos. 1972). Note, for example, the meaning of *run* in contexts such as *the boy was running* and *the horse was running*. The movement of the feet is different for bipeds and quadrupeds, but there are repeated instances in which no foot is in touch with the supporting surface. It is this distinction that provides a basis for distinguishing between *run* and *walk*. And although relative speed is an important factor, it is not determinative because there can be *stationary running* or *running in place*. Furthermore, some people can walk faster than others can run.

But what is to be done in applying this same definition to the running of a crab along a beach. At least two feet are in touch with the surface at all times, and with *a snake running across the lawn* there are no feet and the body is in continuous contact with the supporting surface. All of these instances of fast movement by an animate being seem to fit together into a type of running, although the different minor distinctions are certainly relevant. All of these movements do, however, seem to belong to the same general class of rapid movement in space by an animate being. But even in these examples the concept of rapid movement in space depends on the combination of *run* and the context of an animate creature.

In causative constructions such as *he ran the horse in the second race*, there are two actions, what the person responsible for the horse actually did in getting the horse entered into the second race, and what the horse did in doing the running.

What, however, is the best way to treat such expressions as *the salmon are running, the blue fish are running, the porpoises are running*? The physical context is water, not land, and there are fins and flippers, not feet. In the statement *the salmon are running* the wider context of what we know about salmon in the Northern Pacific means that vast numbers of salmon are swimming upstream to the very ponds where they were hatched some three or four years earlier. There the salmon return to breed and die.

For the statement *the blue fish are running*, the usual implication is that there are large schools of such fish and that they are biting, and although the porpoises are mammals, not fish, a statement that they are running is parallel to a reference about fish.

In analyzing a series of uses of a word such as *run* should there be a difference based on the context of land versus water? Most speakers of English would seem to agree that this would be significant, but no final decision can be made until all different "uses of *run* in context" can be carefully studied, because there are always marginal uses that do not neatly fit any classification. For example, Americans are very likely to say, *she ran over to the neighbors to borrow some sugar* or *he ran down town to get some more icecream because so many more people came to the picnic*. It would be extremely rare for either the woman or the man to have actually run. The first statement focuses more on the short period of time, and in the second sentence the man would presumably have taken a car to go to town. These two uses of *run* focus on the brief period of time and not on the actual physical movement.

But *run* may also occur in a number of additional contexts, for example, *the clock is running, his heart is running, the machine is running, the car is running*. These sentences involve different types of internal, and usually mechanized, running, since even in the case of the last sentence, namely, *the car is running*, the reference is normally not to the movement of the car but to the movement of the engine left running.

In the context *he ran the car down the hill* there are also two activities, the driving and the movement of the car, in which case the first may be regarded as causative and the second as participational, but there are also other different kinds of running, for example, *the water is running, the faucet is running, his nose is running, the flour is running out of the bag*, in which there is a movement of a mass, either liquid or dry. The use of *faucet* or *nose* is obviously an indirect reference to a liquid mass.

For contexts about more or less scheduled transportation by vehicles, the verb *run* has been traditionally employed, for example, *the bus runs between the end of Manhattan and 125th Street, a fast train runs each day from Chicago to San Francisco, a Cunard Line ship runs regularly between New York and Cherbourg*. But until twenty years ago most Americans in the Northeast spoke of commercial airplanes as *flying* from one place to another. Gradually, however, people are more frequently using the verb *run*, especially for frequent, scheduled trips, for example, *a plane runs every hour on the hour from New York to Washinton D.C.*

The verb *run* may also refer to extension, for example, *the play ran for three months, the line ran off the page, the bill ran to sixty dollars, the rose bush ran along the fence."* In all of these instances *run* combines with words to refer to extent of time, space, or quantity. The final example, namely, *the rose bush ran along the fence*, may refer either to a state or to a process of growth, but in all of these typical uses of *run* the meaning is a combination of *run* and the context. And the context obviously contributes far more to the resulting concept than the verb *run*. Accordingly, it would seem wise to regard the various occurrences of *run* as instances of molecular meaning, rather than of atomic meaning. Instead of treating the verb *run* as having a hundred or so meanings, with different words in the context pointing to the right meaning, it seems much better to regard the appropriate lexical unit as consisting of the verb *run* plus the context. In other words, instead of thinking of *run* and the context as two atomic units, it would appear much more realistic to combine the verb *run* and the context into a "semantic molecule."

In addition to these frequently occurring examples of *run* in various contexts, there are a number of minor types, for example, *the dye is running, the color is running* (a reference to loss of color or discoloration), *the boulder ran down the hill, the loose hubcap ran into the ditch* (movement caused by gravity or thrust), *he ran two thousand copies of the book* (a matter of publication), *they ran him in the spring election* (a process of being elected to a political position), *a run on the stock exchange* (an overwhelming demand for liquidation of assets), *the cow ran dry, the well ran dry* (a process of change of state), *he ran 2,000 head of cattle on his ranch* (a reference to pasturing), *the business runs very efficiently* (management of an institution), *her stocking is running, the sleeve of his sweater has a run in it* (a reference to the unravelling of knitted wear).

Although the above occurrences of *run* together with different types of contexts are not exhaustive, they do illustrate certain important advantages over the traditional tendency to consider a verb such as *run* as having an inherent number of meanings and the contexts only pointing to the correct interpretation. It is not only more relevant to recognize the important role of the contexts, but especially for translators it is also more significant to consider both the focal term and the contexts as constituting molecular units. It would be a mistake, however, to insist that such a molecular approach to lexical meaning is the only way to deal with multiple semantic uses of terms.

The verb *run* occurs in a number of partial and complete idiomatic structures with *into* and *down* (Makkai, 1972). In the statement *John ran into the house* the component *ran into* may be understood in a completely literal sense if John was physically running and ended up inside the house. But if the context shows that John was in a car at the time he ran into the house, then *into* is not used in its literal sense of being within an enclosure but indicates impact, in which the car would normally be more damaged than the house.

But it is also possible to say *on the first day of the convention John ran into his friend Jim in the publications section*. The chances are that John was not actually running but simply encountered his friend in unexpected circumstances. Since the likelihood is that John was not actually running, the combination *ran into* needs to be treated as a full idiom, because neither component of the phrase is to be understood in its normal sense.

In the statement *he ran down the hill* both components *ran* and *down* are no doubt to be understood in their literal meanings, but in the sentence *they ran down the opposition with scurrilous propaganda* the combination *ran down* is clearly an idiom. On the other hand, the statement *they ran down the criminal* may be a semi-idiom if the criminal was chased and finally caught, or a complete idiom if *ran down* refers merely to identification.

The verb *run* may also refer to extension in the context *the road runs along the ridge of the mountains*, but this usage overlaps somewhat with the concept of shape in talking about entities, for example, *the road winds through the valley, the road follows the bends in the river, the road turns just beyond the bridge.*

Some verbs, however, are primarily only markers of so-called "voice," as in the case of *make* used as a causative: *the captain made the men run through the woods, he made a liquid into a solid* (cause to become or happen), *he made a good statesman* (become), *the ship made port* (cause to be at an appropriate place or state), *make believe* (cause to be considered true), *make a speech* (cause to happen), *make sense* (cause to be meaningful in some context).

The context not only determines how a word is to be understood, but also how it is to be translated. For example, in Chinese terms for "fish" and "water" do not "run." When a "fish runs" it "disappears," and when "water runs" it "leaks."

Some people find it helpful to study distinctions in meaning in sets of words having the same initial component, for example, the element *out-* in the series *outcast, outclass, outcrop, outdo, outline, outlook, outfit, outlast, outlaw, outpost, outrank, outsell, outvote, outwit*, in which there are two quite different semantic functions of *out-*: (1) beyond certain limits, either physical or sociological, *outcast, outcrop, outlook, outlaw, outpost* and (2) beyond an expected degree: *outclass, outdo, outrank, outsell, outvote, outwit*. But the terms *outfit* and *outline* do not seem to fit either category.

Other people find it interesting and helpful to study series of phrases having one component the same, but with quite different meanings for the key combinations. An excellent set of examples of molecular units includes *soft egg* (only partially cooked), *soft music* (low volume of sound), *soft touch* (either touching a surface lightly or a person who can be easily appealed to for help), *soft spot* (an area that yields readily to touch), *soft drink* (an effervescent, nonalcoholic beverage), *soft focus* (a photograph with somewhat indistinct lines), *soft heart* (generous attitude), *soft pedal* (to understate certain differences), *soft sell* (selling without putting on pressure to buy), *soft spoken* (low volume of speech), *software* (computer program), *soft wood* (wood from nondeciduous trees, which may actually be harder than the wood of some deciduous trees).

These various types of syntagmatic contexts represent the principal means by which most people learn the meanings of at least 95% of their active and passive vocabulary. In fact, many people have a vocabulary of 25,000 words or more, without ever having looked up a word in a dictionary. But these syntagmatic types of contexts are only one of several kinds of contexts that are relevant for understanding the meaning of a text.

3.1.2 Paradigmatic contexts

In many instances, however, it is important to determine the meanings of terms on the basis of contrasts and comparisons with the meanings of related words within the same paradigmatic set, for example, *talk, whisper, babble, murmur, stutter, sing, hum.* These seven terms all belong to the domain of noise produced by speech organs, but there are also very clear distinctions in meaning, based on such features as verbalization, musical pitch, repetition, and voicelessness.

The word *talk* is the most common term and may be characterized as verbal, nonmusical, and alternating between voicing and voicelessness. But *whisper* generally refers to speech in which the vocal cords do not vibrate, except in the case of *stage whisper* (used in dramatic performances) in which there is a vibration of the vocal cords but also heavy breathiness that gives the impression of lack of vibration of the vocal cords. *Babbling* is a type of pseudoverbal performance, with alternating voicing and voicelessness, while *murmur* is masked, low-volume speech. The term *stuttering* designates a kind of speech in which phrase-initial consonants or syllables are repeated several times and often the meaning of the utterance is largely masked. *Singing*, however, involves both verbalization and musical pitch, while *humming* is nonverbal but has musical pitch.

Various types of self-propelled movement, for example, *march, dance, walk, hop, skip, jump*, may also be described in terms of certain distinctive features. For example, *march* is walking rhythmically, usually in company with other persons, while *dance* is also rhythmic, but involves a number of different possible movements of the feet and legs (as well as torso, arms, hands, and head in some cultures). The meaning of *walk* implies various types of movement in space by alternating movements of the lower limbs, although it is possible to mimic this movement by walking on one's hands.

Hopping normally involves only one foot at a time, and *skipping* involves a double forward movement, first with one foot and then with the other, and *jumping* may involve both feet at the same time or with a running start a single foot in taking off and one or both feet in landing.

The analysis of meaningful distinctions between words within a single domain can be very helpful in finding precisely the right manner to represent the meaning of a source-language text. But there are certain disadvantages in that people do not realize that such meanings seem much more distinctive than their really are. The semantic boundaries of all meanings are fuzzy and indefinite (Nida, 1975).

3.1.3 Contexts involving cultural values

Differences of cultural value are also important factors in understanding a series of related terms, for example, *nigger, negro, colored, black* and *Afro-American* representing in each instance a desire to avoid or to employ expressions that are culturally insulting. Unfortunately, however, in some instances substitutes are misleading. For example, *janitors* in universities are often called *building engineers* so as to avoid depreciating the activity of people who sometimes make more money than do the professors. But the terminology can also be misleading.

The typical vocabulary of certain occupations also carries important information about status and behavior, for example, the professional dialects of lawyers and doctors, who often seem to use words to reinforce their social status rather than to communicate important information to clients. But the dialects of the Mafia in Europe and the Triads in Asia have an added purpose of not being understandable to persons that are not a part of the group.

Dialects are often described as being horizontal if they refer to people living in different areas, for example, Cockney vs. Midlands dialect in Great Britain and in New England *Bah Hahbah* for *Bar Harbor*. Such differences are often employed in novels to highlight distinctions in social class.

In many respects the vertical sociolinguistic dialects are even more significant since they carry so much information about the education and social class of participants. Compare, for example, southern Appalachian *you'unz* and *y'oll* for *you all* in standard English. Sociolinguistic dialects are extremely important in some novels since the deviations from standard usage often serve to mark more honest, reliable characters. In traditional American society farmers are usually regarded as more upright that city dwellers.

Correct technical terminology also serves to mark a statement as reliable and the writer as knowledgeable, for example, terms in computer technology, *enhanced mode, mouse, back-up files, cartridge fonts, antivirus, autoexec.bat files, compressed drives, directory tree, doubleclick, erase command, floppy disks* (even when disks are no longer floppy), *laptop, memmaker, menudefault, notepad, online help, optimizing windows, program manager, scrolling, keyswap file*. But correct terminology also serves as a context for highlighting technical content and providing a basis for recognizing the possible technical meanings of other words.

Some terms may simply serve to suggest emotive responses. For example, in American English such words as *nation, apple pie, mother, stars and stripes* provide a positive emotional setting, while for most people words such as *junky, garbage, bastard, punk, slut* are emotively negative, but speakers may differ radically about the emotive values of such words as *communism, socialism, free enterprise, homosexual.*

3.1.4 Contexts that favor radical shifts in meaning so as to attract attention

Figurative meaning is a frequent technique to attract attention. For example, the term *delicious* in the phrase *delicious idea* has nothing to do with taste, but with a pleasurable attitude toward some concept. Likewise, a travel agency in Brussels attempts to attract customers by means of a sign *Stop and Go.*

Some contexts, however, require expressions to provide meaning without stating precisely what is involved. When an investigator sought information from the Sorbonne University in Paris about a professor from the Middle East who was supposed to be extremely poor, the clerk in the department of personnel could not give a direct answer, because this would be ethnically unacceptable, and so she remarked, "He has an apartment in the Continental Hotel," which at that time was the most expensive hotel in Paris. Nothing more needed to be said.

Most proverbs also occur in contexts that show that they should not be understood literally. The West African proverb about "People who hunt elephants never sleep cold" is not about the benefits of firewood left by elephants that break down trees to feed on the leaves, but about undertaking difficult tasks so as to have many supplementary benefits.

3.1.5 The context of a source text

The meaning of a text may depend in large measure on some completely different text, often spoken of as a process of intertextuality. For example, *out damned spot* and *to be or not to be* immediately suggest Shakespeare, and *verily, verily* and *hallelujah* sound like the Bible. The writer of the biblical books of First and Second Chronicles obviously depended for much of the content on other Old Testament books, especially First Samuel through Second Kings. What is particularly interesting is the fact that in Second Samuel 24.1 it is the Lord God who urged King David to number the people of Israel, but in 1 Chronicles 21.1 it is Satan who is responsible for this tragedy. Such a difference has important theological significance, especially since the Books of the Chronicles were written after the return from exile in Babylon.

3.1.6 The audience of a discourse as context

The audience of a discourse also serves as a context to highlight the meaning. For example, the parable of the Father and Two Sons in the Gospel of Luke, Chapter 15, there are two audiences: the repentant outcasts who gladly listened to Jesus and the Pharisees who were suspicious of Jesus and had contempt for the outcasts. The differences in the audience parallel closely the experiences and behavior of the younger and older sons. The parable is really about the goodness of God, which the outcasts accept, and about self-righteousness, that is never reconciled to the God of the New Testament.

3.1.7 Different characters and circumstances in a discourse as contexts for different language registers

The different registers employed in a discourse, namely, ritual, formal, informal, casual, and intimate, often serve as diagnostic devices to mark different sociological relations between the characters of a novel or degrees of presumed identity between speakers and audiences. Close friends rarely use formal language in speaking to one another, but as a plot develops a change in register between persons can be a highly meaningful device.

In some cases, however, the level of language does not seem to match the vocabulary of the presumed audience. The French newspaper *Le Monde* is generally leftist in its interpretation of the news and would seem therefore to appeal to the less educated segment of the French proletariat, but the high stylistic level of language in both vocabulary and grammatical structures is decidedly upper class. This disparity shows that in reality the newspaper is directed to intellectuals and not to the average French speaker.

3.1.8 The imprecise content of a text as the context for symbolic language

The symbolic language of lyric poetry and religious expression seems to be a direct result of the imprecise nature of lyric poetry, and especially so of religious poetry. Note the following brief poem by Emily Dickinson:

> *My Life Closed Twice*
>
> My life closed twice before its close;
> It yet remains to see
> If Immortality unveil
> A third event to me.

So huge, so hopeless to conceive,
As these that twice befell.
Parting is all we know of heaven,
And all we need of hell.

3.1.9 The content of a text as a context for phonetic symbolism

The phonetic symbolism in words is a powerful device for reinforcing the meaning of a text, and perhaps more than any other poet, Edgar Allan Poe employed phonetic symbolism as a means of establishing a contextual relation between verbal sounds and semantic content. Compare, for example, the third, fourth, and fifth lines in *The Raven*.

While I nodded, nearly napping, suddenly there came a tapping,
As of some one gently rapping, rapping at my chamber door —
" 'Tis some visitor," I muttered, "tapping at my chamber door —
Only this and nothing more."

And in the first stanza of *The Bells:*

Hear the sledges with the bells —
Silver bells!
What a world of merriment their melody foretells!
How they tinkle, tinkle, tinkle,
In the icy air of night!
While the stars that oversprinkle
All the heavens seem to twinkle
with a crystalline delight;
Keeping time, time, time,
In a sort of Runic rhyme,
To the tintinnabulation that so musically wells
From the bells, bells, bells, bells,
Bells, bells, bells —
From the jingling and the tinkling of the bells.

Or consider the effective use of phonetic symbolism in the first and third sentences of *The Fall of the House of Usher*:

"During the whole of a dull, dark, and soundless day in the autumn of the year, when the clouds hung oppressively low in the heavens, I had been passing alone, on horseback, through a singularly dreary tract of country, and at length found myself, as the shades of evening drew on, within view of the melancholy House of Usher...I looked upon the scene before me — upon the mere house, and the simple landscape features of the domain — upon the bleak walls — upon the vacant eye-like windows — upon the few rank sedges — and upon a few white trunks of decayed trees — with an utter depression of soul which I can compare to no earthly sensation more properly than to the after-dream of the reveler upon opium — the bitter lapse into everyday life — the hideous dropping off of the veil."

Note the unusually high number of *s*-like sounds and the repeated use of nasal consonants, as well as the frequency of *d* and *r*.

The preceding types of contexts are not exhaustive, but they may serve as some of the more important ways in which a context may lead to certain types of content and reinforce the meaning and form of a text.

3.2 Range of vocabulary

3.2.1 The level of vocabulary required for translating texts in B and C languages

As already noted in Chapter 1, a high percentage of young people studying to be translators or interpreters have a serious lack of relevant vocabulary in their B and C languages (their primary and secondary foreign languages) and some are inadequate even in their A language (their own mother tongue). As a result, students waste a great deal of time in taking courses in translating and interpreting. In fact, some of the best schools make students pass stiff examinations in such languages before permitting them to study translating, and in some countries translating and interpreting are only graduate courses. Such schools obviously produce much better graduates because they start with more qualified people and therefore do not need to spend a large amount of time in language teaching. Furthermore, programs in translating are not ideal ways to learn a foreign language.

It is, however, impossible to indicate the size of vocabulary that a person needs for translating, because so much depends on the contents of a text and the audience for which a translation is produced. Some people claim that a translator must know a minimum of 50,000 words, but this does not say anything about the active and passive knowledge. The only way to test lexical adequacy is to determine how many times translators need to look up the meanings of words on a typical page of text. If, for example, people have to look up an average of six words per page such persons are clearly not ready to start translating as either free-lance or in-house professionals. Their progress will be so slow that they will never make a living out of their work, and the fact that they must look up so many words means that they are very likely to make serious mistakes in understanding a source text. In order to translate efficiently and accurately translators should not have to look up more than one or two words per page.

Whenever possible a translator should learn to dictate translations that can then be transcribed by a secretary and later reviewed for content and form. By using an oral procedure many translators find that they can proceed more rapidly and often more accurately, since a well-trained translator can usually handle texts with greater stylistic effectiveness in an oral process. Such a procedure, however, also requires considerable practice. But by employing an oral technique some translators can average as many as twenty-five pages of text per day, especially if the contents are somewhat routine, as in the case of stock recommendations or reports to stockholders, but merchandizing texts often require much greater creativity.

Most professional translators try to specialize in certain types of texts, for example, technology, law, merchandising, drama, novels, and history, and they do not hesitate to tell agencies or their employers the subject matter in which they are the more skilled. If an agency offers a text to a translator that is not within his or her area of special competence, the translator should explain that he or she is not fully competent in such a genre, but that a particular friend or colleague could no doubt handle such a text efficiently.

In general, people working in multilingual communication tend to be either translators or interpreters, but some translators find that it is beneficial to also do some interpreting, since it provides excellent opportunities to keep abreast of new developments in specialized fields. And likewise interpreters often benefit greatly from translating since the precision that is required sharpens their interpreting skills.

3.2.2 Expanding a translator's vocabulary

Since 95% of most people's verbal inventory of their mother tongue is learned from syntagmatic contexts, that is, from hearing or seeing words in actual texts, students should follow essentially this same approach for vocabulary enrichment by learning the meanings of words through relevant contexts.

Most good writers provide meaningful contexts for the comprehension and use of unusual terms that they need to employ, whether in technical or literary texts. Carl Sagan's book entitled *Cosmos* (1980) is an excellent source of information about semi-technical vocabulary. A *light-year* is described as the distance light travels in a year, going at the rate of approximately 300,000 kilometers a second, and a *galaxy* is described as composed of gas and dust and stars — billions upon billions of stars, and at least some hundred billion galaxies, each with an average of a hundred billion stars.

On page 24 *organic molecules* are described as "complex microscopic architectures in which the carbon atom plays a central role," and the rest of the page describes how these molecules became the origin and evolution of life. Such information is much more relevant than looking up the words *organic* and *molecules* in a dictionary.

The expression *artificial selection* (p.26) is carefully explained and described as the manner in which people have domesticated plants and animals by controlling their breeding. This process is then contrasted with *natural selection*, the process that has occurred in nature and has formed the basis for the theory of evolution.

On page 31 deoxyribonucleic acid, DNA, is briefly described as the "master molecule of life on Earth," and this is then set in a context of biological mutation. Human DNA is discussed later as "a ladder a billion nucleotides long." And then, after indicating that most of the possible combinations of nucleotides perform no useful function, the text indicates that "only an extremely limited number of nucleic acid molecules are any good for life-forms as complicated as we." Even so, the number of useful ways of putting nucleic acids together is stupefyingly large…probably far greater than the total number of electrons and protons in the universe.

Choroplasts are also described on the same page as "tiny molecular factories…in charge of photosynthesis — the conversion of sunlight, water and carbon dioxide into carbohydrates and oxygen." This is precisely the kind of information that most people need to know, in contrast with the Random House Collegiate Dictionary that describes *chloroplasts* simply as "a plastid containing chlorophyll," and then describes chlorophyll as being of two types, listed with their complex chemical formulas. A well written text is normally far better than a dictionary for learning the meanings of words because a text is usually designed to help people understand words in relevant contexts.

Viroids are discussed (p. 39) as "the smallest living things…composed of less than 10,000 atoms. They cause several different diseases in cultivated plants and have probably most recently evolved from more complex organisms rather than from simpler ones." The text then follows with a description of *viruses* and the smallest known free-living organisms, the pleuropneumonia-like organisms (PPLO).

For persons who wish to expand their passive vocabulary, it is advisable to begin with texts involving subject matter with which the reader is well acquainted or in which he or she has great interest. In this way, the reader can constantly provide contextual information in which such words fit. Technical texts are likely to have more unknown words, unless a reader is particularly well informed about some technical subject

It may also be useful to refine one's knowledge of lexical meaning by making diagrammatic charts about occupational domains, for example, music, in terms of various instruments (cornet, French horn, oboe, violin, cello, bass viol, harp, drums), musicians (players, composers, mixers, singers, conductors), types of music (classical, rock, the blues, gospel, jazz), and locations of performance (nightclubs, concert halls, auditoriums, festivals).

Another important technique for rapid expansion of a particular segment of a lexical inventory is to assemble a number of words belonging to a particular semantic domain, for example, verbal communication, which may contain a number of sub-domains: (1) types of discourse: *report, narration, summary, speech, lecture, article, letter, joke,* etc., (2) voice quality: *yell, shout, grumble, whisper, sing, murmur, hum, etc.*; (3) orthography: *alphabetic, syllabic, ideographic,* etc.; (4) publication units: *book,, brochure, magazine, newspaper, leaflet,* etc.; (5) relations between participants in communication: *converse, argue, debate, entreat, pray, answer, interrogate, apologize.*

One important means of testing proficiency in a foreign language and in expanding a verbal inventory is to write an article in the language and have a mother-tongue speaker go over it for lexical appropriateness, grammatical correctness and style. Such written material should not contain grammatical errors, but the choice of words may be inappropriate to the context and the style is likely to be bookish, rather than natural. Having one's compositions carefully scrutinized and corrected by competent users of a foreign language can be a tremendous advantage. One American teacher with advanced degrees in Spanish from an American and a Mexican university and with more than twenty-five years of experience in Latin America never sends off an important letter or article in Spanish unless it has first been checked by a Spanish speaker. He has never stopped learning Spanish.

Even though a translator may be able to find a rare term in a dictionary, this does not mean that he or she is likely to discover the correct meaning for a particular context, because no dictionary ever contains all the range of usage or defines meaning in completely precise ways. Most competent translators, however, seldom use bilingual dictionaries, since monolingual ones are so much more likely to provide more satisfactory contexts and define meanings in more precise and helpful ways.

When people try to expand their vocabulary rapidly by reading texts in a B or C language, they often depend too much on a dictionary to give them the meanings of unknown words. They should actually try to determine the meanings of words from the contexts, as may be illustrated by the following paragraph from page 76 of the French novel *Je vous écris d'Italie...* "*I write to you from Italy*" by Michel Déon (Gallimard, 1984). The italicized words are those that the reader did not at first recognize, but which he tried to understand by taking the total context into consideration.

> "Beatrice *se cala* dans son siège et eut un geste que Jacques n'attendait pas d'elle: après avoir délacé ses *espadrilles*, elle posa ses pieds nus sur *le tableau de bord*. Le ruban qui enlaçait la *cheville* avait laissé une marque plus claire sur la peau *mate* bien qu'elle eût passé la journée à l'ombre de la tonnelle, à l'ombre de son chapeau de paille qu'elle tenait maintenant *serré* contra sa poitrine, jouant avec les primevères *décousues* par Diva. L'attitude *désinvolte*, inattendue de Beatrice troubla tant Jacques que, *obsédé* par ces pieds nus dont les doigts s'agitaient avec *drôlerie* comme s'ils pianotaient, il pris mal un virage et une deuxième fois manqua de verser dans le fossé."

To understand this paragraph it is first essential to know something about what has preceded. The text tells about an attractive woman with dark skin, named Beatrice, who was responsible for the historical documents and art collection in the Italian town of Varela, and about Jacques, a doctoral candidate who was studying the documents in order to reconstruct the life and history of this 16th Century town. The two had just completed a visit to a farm and were on their way back to Varela on a hot summer afternoon in Jacques' small car. But instead of looking up the underlined words in a dictionary, the reader tried to discover the meaning of the words by considering their contexts, consisting of the immediately surrounding words and of the entire preceding part of the novel.

The verb *se caler* in combination with *son siège* "her seat" suggests "fitting comfortably into her seat" or even "nudging herself into her seat," since the small size of the car has been mentioned earlier in the novel. The rest of the sentence can be rendered as "did something that Jacques had not expected her to do." The French word *geste* is often translated as "gesture," but here the reference is clearly to an action that is not a mere gesture, but a particular act or deed that has special meaning for Jacques — a frequent use of *geste*.

The context about the summer being hot, the trip being made to a farm in the country, and the footwear being untied provides enough context to suggest that the *espadrilles* were probably a kind of "sandals," especially when the following clause indicates that her feet were bare and that she propped them up on the *le tableau de bord*, which could only refer to the dashboard.

The *cheville*, where the ribbon was tied, would no doubt be her "ankle," and the clear mark on her *mate* ("dark") skin would be known from previous contexts, but in view of the ribbon the color would no doubt be even lighter than the skin exposed to the sun. The straw hat had to be held tight (*serré*) against her bosom or it would have blown away.

Beatrice continued to play with the primrose bouquet that had been "messed up" (literally, "unsewn") by Diva, the cat (a fact also known from a preceding context).

The attitude that was unexpected of Beatrice and that troubled Jacques must have been either extremely casual or relaxed (*désinvolte*), because putting feet up on a dashboard and giving the impression of playing a piano with the toes is certainly not normal behavior.

Since the behavior of Beatrice caused Jacques to almost drive into a deep hole, the term *obsédé* must imply a serious effect, for which the English term "obsessed" (a cognate word) would be an appropriate equivalent. The term *drôlerie* looks like the English word *droll*, that often refers to something that is funny in an odd way, in which case the English and French cognates match.

As the result of using several different contexts to determine the meaning or meanings of the underlined words, it is possible to have a correct understanding of the complete text without having to look up all the doubtful or strange terms. A reader can become more and more efficient in deducing the meaning from contexts and at the same time the meanings of the words are much more likely to be remembered in their appropriate contexts. Furthermore, the portion of the text understood by this technique becomes an additional part of the context which in turn can assist in clarifying further unknown terms.

A specialist in teaching English to foreigners always insists that people should dispense with a dictionary if they can follow a text enough to make sense of what is happening. In this way, a person is much more inclined to keep on reading, because nothing is so fatal to a story than having to keep looking up five or six words for every page. As a person reads more and more, the vocabulary makes more and more sense, and reading becomes a substitute for the constant hearing of a foreign language in realistic contexts.

The following Spanish text is from the first part of Miguel de Unamuno's philosopical novel *Niebla* "The Cloud" (Obras Selectas, pp. 855–992, Madreid,

Editorial Plenitud) As can be clearly noted, the vocabulary is much more diverse and the grammatical structures considerable more complex than in the case of the French text, but nevertheless, the contexts serve to make the meaning relatively clear. And as in the case of the French text, only italicized words are discussed.

> Porque Augusto no era un *caminante*, sino un *paseante* de la vida. "Esperaré a que pase un perro — se dijo — y tomaré la dirección inicial que él tome."
>
> En esto pasó por la calle no un perro, sino una *garrida* moza, y tras de sus ojos se fue, como *imantado* y sin darse de ello cuenta, Augusto.
>
> Y asi una calle y otra y otra.
>
> "Pero aquel chiquillo — iba diciendose Augusto, que más bien que pensaba hablaba consigo mismo...¿qué hará allí, tirado de bruces en el suelo? ¡Contemplar a alguna hormiga, de seguro! ¡La hormiga, ¡bah!, uno de los animales más hipócritas! Apenas hace sino pasearse y hacernos creer que trabaja. Es como ese *gandul* que va ahí, a paso de carga, codeando a todos aquellos con quienes se cruza, y no me cabe duda de que no tiene nada que hacer. ¡ Qué ha de tener que hacer, hombre, qué ha de tener que hacer! Es un vago, un vago como...¡No, yo no soy un vago! Mi imaginación no descansa. Los vagos son ellos, los que dicen que trabajan y no hacen sino *aturdirse* y *ahogar* el pensamiento. Porque, vamos a ver, ese *mamarracho* de chocolatero que se pone ahí, detras de ese vidriera, a darle al rollo majadero, para que le veamos, ese exhibicionista del trabajo, ¿qué es sino un vago? Y a nosotros ¿qué nos importa que trabaje o no? ¡El trabajo! ¡El trabajo! ¿Hipocresía! Para trabajo el de ese pobre paralítico que va ahí medio *arrastrándose*...Pero ¿y qué sé yo? ¡Perdone, hermano! — esto se lo dijo en voz alta.... ¿Hermano? ¿Hermano en qué? ¡En parálisis! Dicen que todos somos hijos de Adán. Y éste, Juanquinito, ¿es también hijo de Adán? ¡Adiós, Juanquín! ¿Vaya, ya tenemos el inevitable automóvil, ruido y polvo! ¿Y qué se adelanta con suprimir así distancias? La manía de viajar viene de *topofobía* y no de *filotopía*, el que viaja mucho va huyendo de cada lugar que deja y no buscando cada lugar a que llega. Viajar...viajar...Qué *chisme* más molesto es el paraguas... Calla, ¿qué es esto?"
>
> Y se detuvo a la puerta de una casa donde había entrado la *garrida* moza que le llevara *imantado* tras de sus ojos...

Although the terms *caminante* and *paseante* are often translated into English by the same term, Unamuno clearly wanted to emphasize the difference between *caminante*, suggesting vehicular, fast travel, and *paseante*, suggesting walking and slower movement, as well as concern for life's meaning, as indicated in the context.

The term *garrida* is relatively rare, but in combination with *moza* "maid," it must refer to attractive appearance, for she is the person whom Augusto follows for several blocks, as though magnetized (*imantado*, derived from *iman* a substance that magnetizes iron).

The meaning of *gandul*, often used in the sense of lazy loafer, is almost defined by the following phrases that speak of such a person as a vago elbowing (*codeando*) everyone and actually having nothing to do. In fact, such people are stunned, bewildered (*aturdirse*) and smothered, choked (*ahogar*), while Augusto's imagination never rests.

The term *mamarrachos* is rare (it is not even cited in the lexicon of María Moliner) but its meaning is made clear by the statement about such a person being an exhibitionist, not a worker. He likes to show off by being in the front window of a chocolate shop with a rolling pin to roll out candy. By way of contrast the text speaks of a poor paralytic who must drag himself along (*arrastrándose*).

Two words in this text were evidently made up by Unomuno, famous as a professor of Greek and philosophy. The term *topofobía*, which is explained in the following clause as "fleeing from each place" (*huyendo de cada lugar*) and *filotopía*, as "concern for each place to which one arrives" (*cada lugar a que llega*).

Finally, the text returns to the umbrella as the most troublesome gadget (*chisme*) of all, and the first sentence of the next paragraph repeats the reference to the attractive maid (*la garrida moza*) and the magnetic attraction (*imantado*).

Although many authors attempt to suggest the meaning of rare words by placing relevant terms in a context that precedes an unusual and crucial expression, Unomuno uses almost exactly the opposite technique, namely, the rare expression is later defined or explained by the following context (the same order is used in a good deal of scientific writing). This means that language learners who think they must constantly look up in order every unknown term in a dictionary are largely wasting time and depriving themselves of the opportunity to learn the meanings of words by means of contexts.

Rapid acquisition of the basic vocabulary of any language can be acquired by concentrating on the syntagmatic contexts, whether oral or written, but narrative texts are much more likely to have fewer highly specific meanings and the relations between sentences are likely to express more evident relations of cause-effect ("and so"), purpose ("in order to"), condition ("if...then"), concession ("although...nevertheless"), temporal sequence ("and then"), while essays that occur in the editorial sections of newspapers are usually more difficult to follow. For example, in the Frankfurter Allgemeine Zeitung, p.7, March 22, 2000 there is an interesting article about the issue of increasingly inadequate supplies of water throughout the world.

As in the case of the French and Spanish texts, a student with a practical use of conversational German for traveling in Germany was asked to mark the number of words that were either unknown or dubiously recognized. The total number of such words was 32, a proportion that is entirely too high for about 180 words of a text. In fact, the student indicated clearly that he was not able to read a newspaper in German. This means that the technique recommended for the texts in French and Spanish could not be applied to this German text because the proportion of known words was too limited to apply to this newspaper essay. In such circumstances it is necessary to use a dictionary, but in a highly selective manner.

First it is important to obtain a standard bilingual dictionary with both definitions as well as glosses. A person should then write in the margins (or in brackets in the case of an electronic text) the presumably correct interpretation of the specific words, but the entire text together with the necessary notations about meanings should be reviewed carefully each day for at least three or four days so as to help a person remember the previously unknown words. But these meanings must always be reviewed in terms of the meaning of each relevant context so as to benefit from the syntagmatic reinforcement of meaning.

The review of this same Frankfurter Allgemeine text by another person indicated nine terms for which the meaning was unknown or doubtful, but for which the context seemed to provide adequate contextual assistance. These words are italicized and numbered within square brackets and are discussed in a following section.

Der Wert des Wassers
Das zweite Weltwasserforum in Den Haag
Die Bewohner vieler westlicher Länder leben so, als stünde ihnen eine unendliche Menge Wasser zur [1] *Verfügung*. In der Dritten Welt hingegen haben derzeit eine Milliarde Menschen keinen Zugang zu sauberem Trinkwasser, und drei Milliarden müssen ohne ausreichende sanitäre Einrichtungen leben. [2] *Wasserknappheit* herrscht in 26 Ländern, nach Schätzungen könnten es im Jahr 2050 schon 66 Staaten sein. Die Weltwasserkommission, eine Gruppe von bekannten Politikern und [3] *Fachleuten* unter der Leitung des stellvertretenden Weldbank-Präsidenten Serageldin, spricht deshalb auch schon von einer weltweiten "Wasserkrise." Wachse die Weltbevölkerung in den nächsten fünfundzwanzig Jahren um zwei Milliarden, dann benötige man siebzehn Prozent mehr Wasser zur [4] *Bewässerung* in der Landwirtschaft, zwanzig Prozent mehr für die Industrie und siebzig Prozent mehr in den Haushalten, rechnet die Kommission vor. Das seien noch [5] *zurückhaltende* Schätzungen, heisst es in ihren jünsten

Bericht. Hinzu kommt, dass viele Gewässer heute schon unbrauchbar sind, weil sie von Industrie und Landwirtschaft verschmutzt wurden.

[6] *Angesichts* solcher Prognosen erscheint es verwunderlich, dass die internationale Politik sich erst [7] *allmählich* für das Thema zu interessieren beginnt. Wärend über andere globale [8] *Umweltbelange* schon seit längerem Diskutiert wird, war Wasser bislang meist nur ein Teilaspekt. Das zweite Welt-wasserforum, das seit Freitag in Den Haag stattfindet, soll diesen [9] *Missstand* beseitigen. Mehr als 3500 Teilnehmer, 158 Delegationen und 155 Minister aus aller Welt, trafen in der niederländischen Haupstadt zusammen, um über Möglichkeiten eines besseren Wassermanagements zu beraten.

1.   *Verfügung* in this context that speaks of an "endless supply of water" must suggest availability, for example "at their disposal" or "for their use," in which case the entire first sentence of the text may be rendered as "The inhabitants of many western countries live as though they had an endless supply of water at their disposal."

2.   Even though a person may not recognize the meaning of *knapp* in the com-pound *Wasserknappheit* as referring to something "scarce" or "barely suffi-cient," the contrast between the first and the second sentence and the fact that the third sentence verifies the second, the term *Wasserknappheit* must refer to insufficient supplies of water. In fact, the term *knapp* may reflect a measure of phonetic symbolism.

3.   The commission for water throughout the world is described as consisting of a group of political leaders and *Fachleute,* who must be the experts, as in the case of any important international convention — never representatives of the well informed public. Furthermore, the component -*leute* is a common term for people and *Fach* is often used for a specialty or profession.

4.   *Bewässerung* is simply a nominal derivative of the verb *bewässern* referring to the use of water (*Wasser*) for some purpose, for example, irrigation, as in this context. Some people may be misled by the umlaut *ä* in the verb construction.

5.   The participial form *zurückhaltende,* based on the corresponding verb mean-ing "to hold back" or "to withhold" relates to the evaluations (*Schätzungen*), men-tioned in the most recent notice, namely, that much of the available water is unus-able as the result of contamination by industry and agriculture.

6.   The preposition *angesichts,* containing the noun *Gesicht* "face," is a com-mon means of saying, "in view of" or "as the result of," referring in this context to the prognoses already mentioned in the first paragraph. In a number of lan-guages such linking words seem difficulty to remember since they occur in so

many different contexts and the referents are not so picturable.

7.   The adverb *allmählich* refers to "slow, steady progress," but such a beginning of interest was obviously rather slow because of the apparent abundance of water. Perhaps this is, however, a case of wishful thinking, because the history of concern for water would seem to be better characterized by the phrase *am Ende* "at last."

8.   The *Umweltbelange*, a compound combining a well-known term *Umwelt* "environment" and *Belange* "the important aspects," of which water was previously only one aspect or part (*Teilaspekt*) of the environment.

9.   The word *Missstand* looks like a typographical error, but it is derived from *Miss* "bad, wrong" and *Stand* "position," or in this context even "point of view" is "set aside" (*beseitigen*).

As should be quite evident from the above analyses of various German words and their relation to contexts, some of the difficulties experienced by English speakers occur because they are unaccustomed to the writing of semantically and grammatically complex compounds. The umlauting of certain vowels, especially in combination with suffixes containing a high front vowel such as *i*, is also confusing, although the rules for such umlauting should have been readily noted at a much earlier stage in learning German.

CHAPTER 4

Relations between words

Professional translators are usually so concerned with the meaning of a text that they seldom give much thought to the grammatical structures of source or receptor languages, because their task is to understand texts, not to analyze them. If, as already mentioned, translators thoroughly understand a source text, they do not need to worry about whether to use nouns, verbs, and adjectives in a particular order so as to represent the meaning. These decisions are made almost automatically.

Similarly, when people wish to express some complex concept in their own mother tongue, their brains quickly and in a largely automatic manner sort out the appropriate kinds of words and arrange them in effective combinations. If a translator adequately controls both source and receptor languages, translating is essentially no different from writing.

As the result of inadequacies in their B and C languages, students of translation must struggle to find the right words and to arrange them appropriately. As a result, their translations frequently seem unnatural, awkward, or even misleading. Such difficulties often result from misleading grammatical terminology and from grammatical systems that are largely unrelated to meaningful relations between words.

4.1 Misleading grammatical terminology

Traditional grammatical terminology is often more confusing than helpful. For example, the so-called possessive construction in English seldom refers to actual possession. Even in the case of *his car* the bank may own more of the car than the one who is said to possess it. Essentially the same problem exists in the phrase *his house*, because the phrase may refer to any place that a person regularly lives, whether owned or not and whether an apartment, a townhouse, or a duplex. The meaningful relations are even more complex in the case of *his leg*, which, though seemingly possessed, is actually a part of the person and not something that is regularly bought or sold.

The phrase *his father* involves a biological relation of direct descent of one generation, and if anyone metaphorically possesses the other, then it would be the father who possesses the son. But the phrase *his wife* suggests quite a different relationship, especially in a monogamist society in which women have full legal rights. Any person who does not distinguish clearly the different sociological relations between the components of *his car* and *his wife* will soon be on the way to the divorce court.

The relation between a so-called possessive pronoun or noun and the following noun may be one of participation in an activity. For example, *his work* is normally a reference to the fact that "1 does 2," whereas the phrase *his punishment* means that "some one does 2 to 1." Many expressions imply an unmentioned activity, for example, *his boss*, in which "2 controls the activity of 1" or *his partner* in which "1 and 2 are related in some joint activity."

In fact, speakers of some languages refuse to translate literally a phrase such as *his God*, because they insist that no one can own God, although they can "worship God" or "trust God." Some relations, however, are unusually complex. For example, in the case of *his heir* the relations may need to be explained as "1 has designated 2 as the person to receive something of value after the death of 1."

The phrase *his memory* is ambiguous because it can refer to the contents of the memory or to the faculty of remembering. But in some instances the head word qualifies an action, as in *his folly* "1 does something that proves to have the characteristic of being 2." But in some instances a phrase may be both ambiguous and obscure if the meaning of the head word is ambivalent, for example, *his party*, which may refer to "a political party of which 1 is a member or which 1 controls," but it may also refer to "a social occasion paid for by 1 or arranged by others as a tribute to 1."

But where does the information come from to make such decisions? As in the case of the meanings of words, discussed in Chapter 3, such information can only come from the larger context. This often means that it is impossible to understand a sentence without considering the nearby paragraphs or even an entire text. For example, the phrase *his old servant* is essentially ambiguous because *old* can refer to the age of the person who serves or to the length of time that the person has served, or to both the age and the time of service. The actual meaning within a particular text can only be resolved by knowing the way in which such words occur in the larger contexts.

In legal texts it is particularly important to recognize inherent ambiguities so as not to translate wrongly or in such a way as to create more problems. For example, the statement *his recent title to the property* may imply that the title was only recently acquired or it may mean that a person had the title to the property up to a recent point of time but no longer. Such ambiguities are the life blood of the legal profession.

Such possessive constructions are, however, only a small part of the semantic problems posed by inadequate terminology used to describe or refer to grammatical relations. For example, grammarians have traditionally treated subject-predicate constructions as meaning "1 does 2 to 3," as in *John hit Bill, John heard Bill.* The formula "1 does 2 to 3" is appropriate for *John hit Bill,* but not for *John heard Bill,* because in the latter expression it is Bill who makes a noise that affects John.

But the statement *John knew Bill had left* implies that the statement *Bill had left* is the content of what *John knew.* Similarly the statements *John said Bill had left, John saw the bridge give way,* and *John felt the animal tremble* are perhaps best treated by considering the predicates *Bill had left, the bridge give way,* and *the animal tremble* as the contents of the preceding verbs. It is then also possible to extend this content relation to include predicate noun phrases, as in *John told the story, John heard the report, John knows the answer.*

Traditional grammars of English speak of certain verbs as "main verbs" and of others as "complements," in such expressions as *they began to work, they stopped digging, they continued to explore the cave,* but semantically the verbs *began, stopped, continued* are really only aspects of the semantically more relevant verbs *work, dig, explore.* In fact, in many languages aspects of activities are indicated by enclitics or affixes attached to verbs.

4.2. Referential grammatical classes

Many inexperienced translators think of grammatical classes of words as being nouns, verbs, adjectives, adverbs, pronouns, prepositions, conjunctions, etc. And they often assume that in translating faithfully they should match these classes in the receptor language. Accordingly, nouns should be translated by nouns, verbs by verbs, and adjectives by adjectives, but such a procedure almost invariably leads to unnaturalness and even perversion of meaning in a receptor language. These traditional grammatical classes are based primarily on the forms of words and their distribution in sentences. In fact, much of the grammatical terminology is derived from the way in which ancient rhetoricians described Greek and Latin.

But in order to understand the meaning of grammatical relations, it is more important to consider the referential classes which reflect more closely the semantic functions of the referents: entities (*boy, tree, house, lake, sky crowd*), activities/events (*think, eat, talk, walk, ride, swim*), states (*dead, tired, sick, angry, happy*), processes, as changes of state and characteristics (*sicken, recover, grow, widen, enlarge*), characteristics of the preceding classes (*tall, round, slow, recent, small, perhaps, good*), and connectors, words that connect words to one another, either coordinately, by means of conjunctives or disjunctives (*and, or, but, except*) and by means of transitionals (*nevertheless, moreover, accordingly*) or subordinately by means of prepositions (*in, around, during, for, by through, beyond*) and conjunctions (*because, in order to, although, where, when, if*).

This focus on the referential classes of words rather than on the formal or distributional features is a great advantage for translators since it forces them to think in terms of what is actually happening in a text. For example, *environmentally damaging waste* and *congressionally guaranteed subsidy* consist formally of an adverb, a participle, and a noun. But the adverbs *environmentally* and *congressionally* actually refer to entities, namely, the *environment* and *congress*. The participles *damaging* and *guaranteed* refer to processes, and *waste* and *subsidy* are entities, but the relations expressed by the two phrases are very different. The phrase *environmentally damaging waste* means that "3 does 2 to 1" while in *congressionally guaranteed subsidy* "1 does 2 to 3."

Analyzing grammatical relations in terms of referential classes is an important tool for unpacking some of the complex combinations of words so that the content may be transferred to a language in which the same content may be expressed by very different grammatical arrangements. Carl Sagan's volume *Cosmos* contains a number of examples of syntactically complex expressions that become much more meaningful when analyzed in terms of referential classes. For example the semantically condensed expression *the revivified thought of ancient Greece* may need to be unpacked in order to understand what is meant. Merely looking in a dictionary for the word *revivify* is not likely to be of much help. One dictionary, for example, defines *revivify* as "to live again, to give new life to, to reanimate," but that is not the sense used by Sagan, who writes about thinking in essentially the same manner as the early Greek scientists, like Anaximander of Miletus, who invented the sun-dial, Hippocrates, who established the medical tradition, and Democritus, who was the first to talk about atoms. Sagan contrasts this early Greek thought with *theological scholasticism*, the way theologians in Western Europe reasoned during the Middle Ages.

In some cases Sagan uses abstract forms of contrast to express more vividly certain distinctions, as in the statement, *schemes which have been accepted by the credulity and welcomed by the superstition of 70 later generations of men*. In order to understand who is doing what, it may be important to think in terms of referential classes and to determine that the *70 later generations of men* include all those people who have lived on earth since then until now. These are the ones who have stupidly accepted the false schemes of thought because of their own superstitions.

Some statements in *Cosmos* are so semantically condensed that they require considerable expansion if their real meaning is to be accurately reflected. For example, the statement *the evolution of life is a cosmic inevitability* is about the development of living creatures out of inorganic compounds as being something that is bound to happen time after time in the cosmos. Although *cosmic* is an adjective, it refers to the cosmos as an entity, and the noun *inevitability* is actually a reference to an inevitable process. Without restructuring the meaning on the basis of referential classes, the meaning of this important statement can be easily overlooked.

Academic texts often require unpacking if the meaning is to be accurately grasped. On one occasion a group of professional translators were asked to consider the sentence, *The reinforcing impacts of natural resource depletion and human destitution are exemplified by trends in the world's farm lands.* This sentence was the first in an article published by an international agency whose avowed purpose was to provide Third World people with helpful information about agriculture and the environment. But the sentence produced an unexpected reaction among the translators. Those working primarily within Indo-European languages insisted that they could translate the sentence, but they also admitted that they did not know what it meant. Other translators working partially in non-Indo-European languages insisted that they would have to understand the meaning of the sentence and only then could they rearrange the constituent parts in such a way as to make sense.

In terms of referential classes the article *the* is a characteristic of definiteness; *reinforcing* suggests repeatedness and causation, while *impacts* are states resulting from the process of *depletion* and from the state of *destitution*. The preposition *of* relates the phrases of process and state to the *impacts*.

The phrase *natural resource depletion* refers to the loss of resources existing in nature, and the phrase *human destitution* refers to people being very poor. These two phrases are combined by the coordinate conjunction *and*.

The passive verb phrase *are exemplified by* points to what follows as being examples of what precedes. *Trends* are only a series of events or states that occur repeatedly, but there is no indication as to any quantitative or qualitative variable. The preposition *in* serves to indicate where such events take place, while *the world's* refers to various parts of the world (there is clearly no possession implied). The term *farm* indicates an activity, and *lands* are entities for farming. But even with all this information it is not possible to determine precisely what the meaning is.

For example, are these *impacts* good or bad (from the immediate context, probably bad)? And is the relation between *depletion* and *destitution* simply a matter of repetition, as suggested by the prefix *re-* of *reinforcing* or is it possibly reciprocal? But as in the case of the meaning of words, the clues to meaning depend on the broader context. Only on the third page of the article does the author finally explain that what is happening more and more in farm lands throughout the world shows how the loss of natural resources results in greater poverty for the people and how their poverty in turn results in increased loss of natural resources.

If translators really understand what a text means, they can usually render it in ordinary language, but this may require technical knowledge and sensitivity to the needs of the intended audience. Some knowledge of linguistics may be useful, as described in the next Chapter, but linguistics is not indispensable, any more than it is for people who wish to write down their thoughts. Translators are communicators of texts, not analysts. If a translator fully understands the meaning of a text, the process of translating it is largely automatic. Expert translators, therefore, let there brains do the work.

But the process of arriving at a fully intelligible understanding of a text may depend not only on the words of an entire text, but also on what the author evidently considered to be the knowledge and concerns of his or her intended audience. Similarly, a translator must ultimately reckon with the presuppositions of those who are supposed to understand a translation. Translators are always juggling several balls at the same time.

The diversity of grammatical constructions and the different ways in which semantic relations between words are expressed often seem bewildering to language learners and even to beginning translators. It may, accordingly, be helpful to shift attention from the details of grammar to some of the basic concepts that can be expressed in all languages, although often in quite different ways.

4.3 Basic meaningful relations between words

Linguists have described in a number of different ways the diverse semantic relations between words on the grammatical level of structure. A translator, however, is not concerned primarily with the nature of the grammatical system, but with the major ways in which referential classes relate to one another in texts. The majority of meaningful grammatical relations between words may be described as attribution, participation, restriction, content, connection, repetition, proportion, and supplementation, but these same semantic relations are also relevant on the level of discourse.

These eight sets of semantic relations are not exhaustive in the sense of including any and all types of relations, but they do represent a general guide to the major types of meaningful relations, and they highlight the fact that there are conspicuously fewer such sets of relations than many people have imagined. They also have a high probability of being widely applicable, even if not universal, in that translators working in several hundred different languages in various parts of the world have not found grammatical relations that do not reflect, at least broadly, these eight sets of relations, which in the following sections will be illustrated primarily by English.

4.3.1 Attribution

In English most attributive constructions consist of three components (1) a subject, normally information shared by speaker and audience, (2) a copulative verb, for example, *be, become, seem, appear*, (3) a predicate element indicating state (*they are tired*), class (*she is a doctor*), characteristic (*the shirt appears red*) or identity (*John Thompson is my colleague*). Apposition is also a type of attribution, for example, *my friend, Bill Jones* and *valleys in the mountains of the brain, convolutions that greatly increase the surface area*.

In a number of languages there is no need for a copulative verb, since the subject and the predicate are linked by juxtaposition, as in Classical Greek and Hungarian. And in some languages, as also in English, there may be an anticipatory pronoun referring to a predicate clause, for example, *it is a shame that he left too early* or a dummy subject, for example, *there was trouble on 47th Street*. In both of these attributive constructions the implied purpose is evidently to treat the entire predicate statement as new information.

4.3.2 Participation

Participation involves a nuclear activity, process or state, and a number of participating satellites: actors (*John ran back*), causers, those who cause something to happen (*John ran his horse in the second race*), affectees (*the man was shot in the back*), instruments (*the key opened the door* or *they used a key to open the door*), indirect affectees (*Jane was given a new car for Christmas*). These satellites may occur in multiple series and in various positions, for example, *the rioters shot the man and then poured gasoline on the car and set it on fire.*

In many Indo-European languages the semantic relation between a verb and different satellites has been traditionally marked by different suffixed case endings, for example, nominative, genitive, dative, accusative, ablative, and vocative, but increasingly these semantic relations are indicated by word order and by prepositions.

4.3.3 Restriction

The process of restriction involves the addition of words that semantically restrict the range of reference of some head expression. For example, the term *men* could potentially refer to some 40% of the world's population, but the addition of *old* in *old men* significantly reduces or restricts the range of reference of *men*. The further addition of preposed and postposed terms, as in *the three old men that talked with me yesterday* radically restricts the phrase *old men*.

The process of restriction is one of the most common types of relations between words, for example, *walked fast* (activity and characteristic), *tired worker* (state and entity), *the dish on the table* (entity and location), *if he works, he must be paid* (condition and activity), *probably escaped* (modal and activity), *continued training* (aspect and activity), *those who arrived late* (entities and activity), *came to help her* (activity and purpose), *an attack late at night* (activity and time). Some linguists include all relations of participation as being restrictions.

In many languages expressions indicating restriction show agreement in number and case with the head word.

4.3.4 Content

Expressions of content occur primarily with verbs of communication, perception, learning, and knowledge: *he said he would return, he saw the thief enter by the back window, the men felt a strange movement coming up through the basement, he learned how to whistle, they all knew that they were condemned to death.* These relations of content may also be analyzed as restrictions, but regarding them as various types of content seems not only structurally justified, but such a classification is useful in treating certain parallel verb-object combinations: *told the story, explained the joke, knew the lesson, sensed her agony of spirit.*

4.3.5 Connection

Connection involves the use of transitionals, conjunctions, and prepositions, in order to link words and groups of words together into larger units.

a. Transitionals

Transitional expressions such as *nevertheless, furthermore, moreover, therefore, next, finally, to conclude* are often semantically equivalent to an entire sentence. For example, the transitional *furthermore* suggests "in addition to what has already been said, it is important to consider the following." Even a word such as *next* at the beginning of a sentence calls attention to what has been said, as well as to the following comment. The transitional *finally* also links the preceding with what follows and marks what follows as the end of a series. The relation of transitionals to what precedes and to what follows is essentially coordinate.

b. Conjunctions

Conjunctions are of two principal types: coordinating and subordinating. The coordinating conjunctions in English are

and (additive)
> *John and Mary*
> *rock and roll*
> *John was in the basement and Mary was in the kitchen*

or (alternative)
> *Mary or Jane*
> *they will finish the work, or at least they will try to finish*

but, except (adversative or disjunctive)
> *he will try but is unlikely to succeed*
> *all but Philip were delighted with the results*

Some coordinating conjunctions occur in couplets: *both...and, either...or, neither...nor*

Some of the principal subordinating conjunctions in English are *so that, in order to, if, although, because, when, while,* for example,

> *he left money so that she could travel*
> *they founded a new company in order to expand into a new industry*
> *we will do it if you pay the cost*
> *although he was sick, he insisted on continuing the journey*
> *no one was drunk when we were there*

The clauses introduced by subordinating conjunctions are all restrictive.

c. Prepositions

Prepositions not only connect sets of words to one another, but they also indicate a wide range of associated meanings: time (*the noise during the night*), space (*the ball under the couch*), agency (*given by a wealthy donor*), cause (*a flood because of spring rains*), extension (*a journey through Egypt*), purpose (*money for a new car*). All of these types of prepositional phrases are restrictive.

4.3.6 Repetition

Repetition generally implies emphasis and in English it may be complete or partial:

> *Yes! Yes!*
> *I like it, I like it*
> *Jane did not go yesterday, she went today.*
> *She wrote the entire poem, not just a part.*

In Bahasa Indonesia, however, the repetition of a word normally indicates plurality, but it is written as a numeral 2 at the end of a word.

4.3.7 Proportion

Expressions of proportion are quite common in all languages, but the structure of such expressions is often quite different. Many depend on contrastive comparative degrees in positive-negative statements. In English comparison is indicated by two related statements of comparative degree, for example, *the more, the better* and *the more he talks the less I believe him*. In some languages, however, comparison consists of a negative-positive set, for example, *John is not friendly, Jim is friendly*, meaning John is less friendly than Jim.

4.3.8 Supplementation

Nonrestrictive pronominal clauses and parenthetical additions are typical ways in which supplementary information may be added to a text without its being structurally related, although it is semantically related. Such expressions are usually set off by punctuation marks in writing and by pause-pitches in pronunciation, for example,

My friend, who hated to sail, nevertheless agreed to go with us through the Caribbean.

Social relations between ethnic groups (this is particularly true of minorities in Europe) are exceptionally complex.

In general the greater the amount of formal marking of grammatical relations for such features as case, gender, number, and dependency, the freer the word order, and conversely the fewer the formal indicators of grammatical relations, the more rigid is the word order, since so much depends on varying types of word order and juxtaposition.

These eight major types of relations between words are, however, of limited application without considering some of the specific ways in which a translator can analyze some of the intricately organized phrases in a language such as English, in which the limited grammatical marking provides a basis for considerable obscurity and ambiguity. Some of these relations can perhaps be best understood by examining some of the most common structures, for example, noun-noun, adjective-noun, and adverbial phrases.

Noun-noun phrases
Some noun-noun phrases are both long and referentially complex, especially if the nouns are nominalized verbs, as in the phrase *acid precipitation assessment program*, in which the terms *precipitation, assessment,* and *program* refer to activities and not to entities. The referential class of *program* is a series of activities, the purpose of which is to assess or evaluate how *acid* (a mass entity) is *precipitated.*

Some semantically complex noun phrases may include an adjective, which may actually refer to an entity, for example, *United States coronary heart disease deaths*. The *United States* is a collective entity, and although *coronary* is formally an adjective, it refers to entities, namely, the arteries in the heart. The term *disease* is a state, and in this context *deaths* is a process. An unpacked restatement of this phrase can be formulated as "deaths of people in the United States caused by disease affecting the arteries of the heart."

In some phrases the same term may occur in quite different combinations, for example, *influenza virus, influenza vaccine, influenza infection*. The phrase *influenza virus* refers to the *virus* that causes the state of *influenza*, but in the case of *influenza vaccine* it is the *vaccine* that prevents *influenza*, while in *influenza infection* the *influenza* is the *infection*.

A seemingly very simple phrase may, however, be completely ambiguous. For example, *fluid transport* may refer to ways in which a *fluid* can be moved from one place to another, for example, by rail, boat, or pipe, but the phrase can also refer to the *transport* of objects by means of a *fluid*, for example, floating logs down a river or piping coal particles mixed with water.

Some noun-noun phrases appear to be descriptions of entities when in reality they are names of a particular type of entity. For example, *mountain laurels*, the name of a medium sized bush growing in the eastern part of North America and in Cuba, is neither a *laurel* nor is it restricted to *mountains*.

The phrases *forest grasses* (grasses that typically grow in forests) and *crown fires* (fires that burn in the crowns of trees) represent a relation of "1 is the place of 2," but in *battle site, customs house* "2 is the place of 1."

Compare also *astronomy satellite* and *tennis racket*, in which "2 is an instrument for doing 1," but in *microscope observations* and *X-ray telescopy* "1 is an instrument for doing 2." Similarly, in *mercury concentrations* and *kidney disorders* "2 is the state of 1" while in *low-density fires* and *mass production* "1 is the state of 2."

For translators trying to understand a source text the real issue is the source of information to provide an understanding of what is involved. Professional translators almost immediately sense the semantic relation in terms of their own background experience, but beginning translators must look to wider encyclopedic sources in order to comprehend the necessary background data.

But as already indicated in Chapter 1 a high percentage of those who produce texts to be made available on political and economic issues for the European Community do not themselves understand the meanings of the documents that they themselves produce. When questioned about the meaning of certain sentences or paragraphs, the common response is "You do not need to know what the text means, just translate it."

In many instances such texts are simply compilations of existing documents in which the meaningful relations between the sections are both obscure and misleading. But this is precisely what translators constantly face, even in the case of texts produced by scientists. One large scientific company found that they had to provide courses for their scientists on how to write accurately and clearly.

Adjective-noun phrases
In some scientific texts adjectives may be semantically very complex. For example, the phrase *paleontological surprise* occurred in a text referring to the surprise experienced by persons who had found fossils associated with a particular paleontological stratum. But the problems of ambiguity are more difficult to handle without special attention being paid to the wider context. For example,

stellar knowledge may refer to remarkable knowledge or to knowledge about the stars, in which case, only the wider context can resolve the ambiguity. But in other instances an adjective may represent a subtle and purposeful oxymoron, as in *patterned chaos*, which is technically a contradiction.

Although some persons assume that the term *kind* in the phrase *kind person* is simply a quality or characteristic of an individual, it is usually a reference to the manner in which a person relates to other people by being kind to them, and in many languages such behavior must be expressed by a verb phrase, for example, "by helping others."

Since adjectives so frequently indicate an essential quality of the following head word, it may be difficult for some persons to realize that often the adjective actually refers to entities, for example, *human needs* are the needs that humans experience, and *ecological shock* refers to what happens to the ecology. In many instances, however, the attributive adjective may refer to the means of doing something, for example, *mathematical analysis* and *chemical treatment*.

In some texts an adjective may refer to entities that engage in certain activities, for example, *interdisciplinary competition* is a reference to the way in which people in different disciplines compete, but in many cases an adjective refers to particular kinds of entities that experience the result of activities contained in the adjectives, for example, *herbivorous dinosaurs* "entities that eat only plants" and *carnivorous animals* "entities that eat only meat."

Literal translations of some adjective-noun phrases can be laughably wrong, for example, *molecular biologists* and *atomic physicists*. The biologists are not molecules nor are the physicists atoms, but in each case "2 studies or works with 1."

Unusual roles of adverbs

Translators from English into other languages are so accustomed to adverbs qualifying events and characteristics, that they sometimes overlook other special relations, as in *intellectually advanced teenagers* meaning "3 is 2 with respect to 1," in other words, "teenagers who are ahead of other young people with respect to intellectual abilities." But the phrase *biologically aggressive role* refers to "activity that proves harmful to other biological species." This phrase summarized the activity of a particular species of birds that greatly diminished the population of another competing species.

Many adverbs qualify complete sentences, for example, *unfortunately, he bled to death* and *paradoxically, such double bonds of fatty acid prove to be less susceptible to oxidation*. In both instances, the initial adverb indicates the nature of the following event. And in many languages it is essential to use a different means of referring to such complete utterances, for example, *he bled to death, this was unfortunate* or *such double bonds of fatty acid prove to be less susceptible to oxidation — something quite contrary to normal expectation.*

Translators do not need to become linguists in order to become first-rate translators, although some study of linguistics can certainly be helpful. But translators must be sensitive to the broader contexts in which words may combine into more and more intricately related sets of grammatical relations. The answer to most problems of meaning come from extended contexts, whether within the text in question or in other texts produced by the same writer or in texts produced by other writers on the same subject, for example, articles in encyclopedias. In the same way that most problems of word meaning depend on the meanings of related words, the meaning of particular grammatical constructions depend on the meaning of related grammatical constructions in other or similar contexts.

CHAPTER 5

Translating texts

Many people have the impression that words are marked by spaces, that grammar is limited by periods, and that discourse refers to the contents of paragraphs. But lexical units may involve entire phrases, for example, *a first-come-first-served arrangement.* Grammars include pronouns that refer backward or forward across sentence boundaries, and discourses may consist of a single word such as *Damn!* or they may even extend to a set of books, for example, the four volumes by Max Gallo on the life of Napoleon. Overlapping the boundaries of words, grammar, and discourse is the name of the game, but the focus of attention for a translator is texts because these are the basic and ultimate units that carry meaning.

Many translators, however, regard features of discourse as being irrelevant to their task as translators, because they think that all they must do is to reproduce the sentences more or less word for word and any problems of the discourse will be automatically accounted for. But this is not the way accurate translating is done. For example, a literal translation of the proverb, "They locked the barn door after the horse had been stolen" would be meaningless in most of the local languages in the equatorial band across Africa. Few people have horses, barns, or locks, but they do have a more clever and sophisticated proverb referring to the chief's son, "They built a bridge over the stream after the chief's son fell in the water."

Some books on translation, however, give the impression that translating means translating languages, rather than texts. They describe the meanings of different semantic domains, list the corresponding grammatical structures, and analyze the distinctive stylistic devices in the respective languages, but this is essentially the linguist's task who analyzes a language from the outside, while a translator needs an insider's view that cuts through the formal differences and deals directly with the meaning of a text to be translated. The foreign words are transformed into concepts, and these concepts become the basis for a translator's producing essentially the same meaning in another language.

Frequently there is a serious error in a text submitted for translation. In a recent report prepared in English by a commission investigating the possibility of

Rumania entering the European Union, there was a reference to a document, presumably prepared by the Rumanian government, in which Rumanian officials were demanding certain reforms in the European Union. The translator of the English document into French readily sensed the inconsistency in the wording. Instead of demanding changes in the European Union, the original document listed changes that the Rumanian government was ready to make in order to become a member of the Union. Accordingly, after discovering what was undoubtedly the real meaning of the document, he adjusted his translation to represent correctly the intent and purpose that lay behind the garbled English text.

Some translators, however, insist that correcting errors is not their business, because their task is to translate what a document says. They insist that if a text is poorly written, they should simply reflect the poor style of the original. Most professional translators, however, either correct obvious mistakes or at least call attention to such matters in a note directed to those responsible for having the translation made.

Most expert translators actually improve the style and organization of a discourse in the process of translating, because they are almost always more proficient in stylistic matters than are the original writers of the documents submitted for translation. For example, when executives in the translation program of the European Union have occasion to compare the same document in various languages, they often find that in one language the form of the document is conspicuously inferior to what it is in the other languages. In such circumstances, the stylistically inferior document is almost always the original.

Mistakes in translation can be readily made if a translator has not read an entire text before undertaking to translate a part. A translation into English of an important lecture in French ended a series of comments on one subject with the statement that the subject deserves further "study and consultation," which the translator assumed referred to the next page. Accordingly, he translated, "as may be noted in what follows." But the translator had obviously not read the next page, which dealt with an entirely different subject.

Unfortunately, many translators are not fully aware of the extent to which well written texts reflect important structural features. The following first paragraph of an article in the Wall Street Journal about *kreteks* in Indonesia illustrates some of the complexity and intricacies of discourse structure:

Kreteks Are Big Business
The kretek is the incense of Indonesia. It is the fragrant haze that chokes visitors as soon as they step off a plane. It is the gray cloud that seems to resonate from the gongs of Javanese gamelan orchestras. It is the strong, aromatic

smoke that fills the lungs of cabinet minister and taxi driver alike. It is the spicy fog that blurs the edges of Indonesia.

Although the explanation about the nature of kreteks (cigarettes made with local tobacco and tiny pieces of hot-burning cloves) is left for the following page, the headline about "big business" will immediate catch the attention of the readers of the Wall Street Journal, and perhaps even more so because they do not know what kreteks are.

The four major sentences are organized in accordance with the temporal sequence in which a person is likely to visit Indonesia: first arriving and being choked by the fragrant haze, then hearing the percussion orchestra that always meets international flights, later noticing the smoke that fills the lungs of everyone, and finally seeing the spicy fog on the edges of Indonesia as his plane flies away.

In addition to the temporal sequence there is also the spatial sequence of the plane, the terminal, the streets, and the edges of Indonesia. The repetition of certain related semantic classes, for example, the series of atmospheric terms: *haze, cloud, smoke, fog,* as well as the distinct odors: *incense, fragrant, aromatic, spicy,* emphasize the unity of the text.

The parallelism of the four sentences beginning with *it is* may seem to some readers as being overdone, but the clever unity of this paragraph, marked by the word *Indonesia* at the end of the first sentence and again at the end of the paragraph highlights the unity of the paragraph. The more readily translators sense the organizational elements of a text, the more relevantly these features can be evaluated and incorporated into a translation.

5.1 Major organizational features of texts

The major organizational features of most texts include time, space, class, connectivity, gradation, dialogue, and literary formulas, constructed out of frequently recurring formal structures. The rapid recognition of such features and their roles in discourses can be a distinct help to translators, who may find that what is excellent for one language-culture does not fit easily into the patterns of other language-cultures. For example, many traditional novels and short-stories in Chinese have unhappy endings, and some publishers of such stories into English have actually changed the endings to make them happy ones, something Americans generally prefer.

Similarly, many discourses in the languages of the Orient do not employ initial topic-paragraphs that state the purpose of a discourse. In fact, topic sentences and topic paragraphs are often regarded as impolite, because they start a section by introducing the conclusion. This seems presumptuous in some cultures, in which speakers or writers first prefer to give all the evidence or reasons for certain conclusions, with the hope that the readers or listeners will come to the proper point of view. But this organization of a discourse seems to many Westerners as simply beating around the bush and disguising one's real intent.

5.1.1 Time

All references to time are essentially linear (time moves only in one direction) and relative, in the sense that time is always being determined by past and future time. Calendrical time is usually based on some important event, for example, the birth of an important person (e.g. AD and BC), a culturally important event (the Hegira for Islam), the period of a particular dynasty (especially in the Orient and in the Middle East), or some great cataclysm, for example, floods or famines.

Good writers and story-tellers are, however, never satisfied with linear time. They insist on flashbacks to fill in a knowledge of important prior events, and they like flash-forwards to suggest that something significant is going to happen later. For this purpose they use such expressions as "as will soon be noted" or "as has happened even until this day," in which the time of a past event is related to the time of the verbal account.

5.1.2 Space

Physical space is normally regarded as consisting of three dimensions: height, breadth, and depth, but in some languages there are other spatial relations that a treated like dimensions, for example, *above, below, behind, in front of, near, around,* etc. Discourse space is generally treated in relation to a communicator, but it may also be related to the position of a dominant character in an account, for example, the location of Jesus in some of the Gospel accounts.

References to space may also occur with verbs of movement, e.g. *come, go, arrive, leave, return, enter, exit,* and the range of meaning in any context may depend on the meaning of still other words. In Hellenistic Greek the verb *erchomai* may mean "come" or "go," but if the verb *hupago* "to go" is in the same context, then *erchomai* can only mean "to come."

Lexical space may depend largely on context. Note, for example, the following English expressions indicating either space or time: *first in line, first to arrive; in front, in time; throughout the land, throughout the night,* as well as verbs and nouns referring to space or time: *approach the village, approach noon; end of the hour, end of the journey.*

Languages may also have spatial systems. In the ancient world of the Middle East the sky was a dome, the earth was flat with a great river encircling it, and the land was supported by subterranean water, but usually with the help of some mythic entity, for example, a huge turtle, a strong hero, or massive columns. The gods inhabited the heavens or tall mountains, and hell or Hades was down because the dead are normally buried in the earth. But spatial orientations may depend largely on local geographical features. For example, Doleib Hill near Malakal in the Sudan is only about three feet higher than the surrounding plain, but it is just high enough never to be inundated by the Nile. Accordingly, it must be a "hill."

Extensive distances must usually be calculated in terms of time, for example, "light years," but in some cultures even short distances are reckoned in terms of time. For example, a particular town may be so many days away, that is, the number of days it takes to walk the required distance. In Switzerland the distance between two points along trails is given in hours and minutes, but in Germany similar spatial distances are given in kilometers.

Nevertheless, translating expressions for space, as well as for time, may involve serious problems if the numbers have symbolic values. The 12,000 stadia of the symbolic New Jerusalem in the Apocalypse is equivalent to about 1,500 miles, but in Judaism and Christianity the number 12 has important meaning, for example, the twelve tribes of Israel and the twelve disciples in the Gospel accounts. Also the 144 cubits (12 x 12) for the height of the wall of the New Jerusalem has important symbolic meaning. But transposing all these symbolic numbers into present-day measurements of space can seriously rob the text of much of its figurative meaning, and for the Apocalypse the figurative values are what count. For such relations some type of footnote is usually required if readers are to understand what is actually involved.

5.1.3 Class

As already noted in the discussion of discourse features of the paragraph about kreteks, the classes of fragrances and atmospheric conditions proved to be significant ways of indicating unity. In addition the use of specific rather than generic language, for example, the reference to *government officials and taxi drivers* as a way of speaking about people in general is important, because terms that are more readily "picturable" always carry more impact.

New types of contexts may, however, change the traditional patterns of grouping entities into classes. For example, in the past a high percentage of people in the Western World made out grocery lists on the basis of the types of objects people wished to buy, for example, meat, fish, vegetables, fruit, bread, etc. At present, however, many people make out lists in terms of the space utilized by shoppers as they go up and down aisles toward the check-out counters.

Some texts, however, purposely violate class expectations in order to describe events symbolically. For example, the first few pages of Claude Simon's novel, *Le Vent* "The Wind" are almost unintelligible because of the broken sentences, the unusual grammar, and the mixed up word order. But soon a reader begins to realize that this is a description of the effects of a whirlwind. The chaotic grammar becomes a metaphor of the contents of the novel.

5.1.4 Connectivity

The connectivity of events is a particularly important feature of narratives, history, and biography, for example, condition, (*if this, then that*), concession (*although this, nevertheless that*), purpose (*do this in order to do that*), result (*because of this, therefore that*). In many texts, however, sequences appear to violate normal patterns of connectivity. For example, Kafka's remarkable novel *The Castle* describes the experiences of a man who must visit the owner of a castle, but he is never able to accomplish his goal. Each episode is almost frighteningly realistic, but the transitions do not make sense. Nevertheless, this is precisely the kind of existentialism that Kafka wished to portray, namely, the realism of experience but the ultimate meaninglessness of life.

The ordering of concepts, as in argumentation, philosophy, and scientific inquiry is even more complex than the sequencing of events. An excellent example of conceptual ordering is found in Sagan's volume *Cosmos*, p. 69.

> Newton discovered the law of inertia, the tendency of a moving object to continue moving in a straight line unless something influences it and moves it out of its path. The Moon, it seemed to Newton, would fly off in a straight line, tangential to its orbit, unless there were some other force constantly diverting the path into a near circle, pulling it in the direction of the Earth. This force Newton called gravity, and believed that it acted at a distance. There is nothing physically connecting the Earth and theMoon. And yet the Earth is constantly pulling the Moon toward us. Using Kepler's third law, Newton mathematically deduced the nature of the gravitational force. He showed that the same force

that pulls an apple down to Earth keeps the Moon in its orbit and accounts for the revolutions of the then recently discovered moons of Jupiter in their orbits about that distant planet.

The first six words neatly state the content of the paragraph, and the rest of the sentence, together with the following sentence, indicates why Newton became concerned with the apparent anomaly involved in the continual circling of the Earth by the Moon. The third sentence is the core of the concept, while the following sentence emphasizes the lack of any physical connection. And the next sentence reiterates what the Earth does, despite the lack of a physical connection.

The last two sentences provide the mathematical basis for gravity and show the practical implications of gravity for ordinary people and an explanation about the new discovery of moons circling around the planet Jupiter. This type of ordering of concepts is what makes Sagan's writing so clear and convincing.

The conceptual world of a particular culture may include hundreds of presuppositions that significantly order the manner in which people reason, and many of these underlying cultural concepts seem almost nonsensical to people in other cultures, for example, the possibility of people turning themselves into fierce animals, the use of black magic to kill a personal enemy, foretelling the future by looking into crystals, guaranteeing the help of the gods by human sacrifice, believing that dishes need to be first washed and then rinsed in water containing fresh cow dung, or determining what a person should do on a particular day by reading one's horoscope in the daily paper.

Some people also have very special ideas about different types of discourse. Many Malayalam speakers in India and Dinka speakers in the Sudan are intrigued with epic poetry, and in some churches in the Philippines, known as *Iglesia ni Cristo*, sermons are accompanied with an emotive dramatization by choruses of weeping women, while in Haiti religious texts about healing can be torn up and made into tea as a cure for any illness.

Some presuppositions, however, seem much more reasonable. For example, saving up for one's old age, chewing the bark of an African yohimbine tree to increase sexual potency, regarding one's reputation after death as one sure kind of immortality, and becoming more and more skeptical about progress in a world that is rapidly outgrowing many of its natural resources. Without the knowledge of the beliefs and practices of other cultures, a translator's perspective of the world is tragically restricted. And it is not surprising that the most serious mistakes in translation are made because of ignorance about the views and values of other cultures.

5.1.5 Gradation

Gradation is a process of increasing or decreasing the intensity of some aspect of a text. For example, a short-story or novel usually contains a series of events in which the characters are faced with increasingly difficult circumstances. But finally, when at the apex of a narrative the hero makes a crucial decision or acts to resolve the crisis, the story unwinds until a new steady state is reached.

Scientific texts may also exhibit series of gradations, often spoken of as "peeling the onion." For example, in the *Scientific American* the first section of an article often describes in more or less ordinary language the importance of some new discovery or technique. A following section describes essentially the same subject matter but in considerably more detail, and frequently there is a final section written primarily for specialists.

Descriptions of landscapes often follow much the same type of gradation but in terms of greater detail and specific features. This type of description, which moves from the broad picture to more intricate elements, is typical of many book reviews and descriptions of personality traits. But the order may also be reversed, and a description may begin with minor details and then move gradually to the larger features.

5.1.6 Reference

Reference consists of two major types: (1) pronominal reference, either referring back (anaphoric) or referring to something ahead (cataphoric), and (2) naming reference, identifying entities and activities by means of proper names.

In place of the traditional triple reference to first, second, and third persons in communication, Navajo has a fourth person, that is, the next third person mentioned in a text. Many languages also distinguish between inclusive and exclusive first person plural, that is, an inclusive *we* referring to the speaker and his audience in contrast with an exclusive *we* that includes the speaker and his associates, but excludes the audience. The wrong use of inclusive and exclusive first person plural has led to many serious problems in litigation.

Proper names are also aspects of reference, because they normally only "refer" rather than "name" classes. But in some languages the same person may have several names, depending on the degree of intimacy between the speaker and the referent. This type of problem often shows up in translations of Russian novels, in which one and the same person may be referred to by four or five different names.

5.1.7 Dialogue

The organization of conversation is primarily a matter of dialogue, in which participants interact in a *yes/no*, a *question/answer*, or a *granted/but* context. In many instances, however, a speaker tries to anticipate the response of an interlocutor and introduces "anticipatory feedback," consciously answering the objections that are likely to come from an audience.

The stream-of-consciousness type of utterance is typical of a person who speaks to himself or herself, and it often contains considerable amount of anticipatory feedback, in which a person tries to answer himself or herself. Such speech is difficult to analyze structurally because it is often impossible to fill in the gaps. Psychiatrists, however, make extensive use of such speech since it indirectly reveals much that concerns a patient and which is so personal as to inhibit a person's supplying such information in a more logical form.

Some people who talk to themselves employ well organized utterances designed to test ideas in front of an imaginary audience. In fact, some people even introduce into their speech possible objections from an imaginary audience.

Prayer is a very special kind of dialogue, in which speech is directed to a supernatural entity, but there is usually no apparent immediate response, although some people insist that God does immediately and audibly answer their prayers by telling them what is to happen and what they must do.

5.1.8 Literary formulas

All cultures have developed ways in which the basic relations between sets of words are organized into a number of general literary formulas, e.g. narratives, conversation, proverbs, puns, epic accounts, animal tales, and poetry (with measured lines and rhythm), and some cultures have a number of specific literary forms, for example, history, short-stories, scientific essays, business letters, contracts, prophecy (speaking about the future and/or on behalf of God), apocalyptic (prophecy about an increasingly bad future until everything is altered by a messiah), and sonnets (the most elaborate and condensed literary form).

Christina Rossetti's poem *Remember* is one of the finest representatives of a centuries-old tradition of sonnet poetry in Western Europe. Note the 14-line pattern in which the first eight lines pose the problem and the last six lines suggest an answer, especially highlighted in the last two lines. The rhyme pattern is also carefully structured as abbaabba and cddfcf. The word *remember* occurs three times in the first eight lines and twice in the six line response, which also includes two occurrences of *forget*. A literal translation of this type of highly structured text would never have precisely the same literary character as the original, but the theme could be reworked into a corresponding sonnet in another language, as a type of "variations on a theme," occurring frequently in music.

Remember

Remember me when I am gone away,
Gone far away into the silent land;
When you can no more hold me by the hand,
Nor I half turn to go, yet turning stay.
Remember me when no more, day by day,
You tell me of our future that you planned;
Only remember me; you understand
It will be late to counsel then or pray.

Yet if you should forget me for a while
And afterwards remember, do not grieve,
For if the darkness and corruption leave
A vestige of the thoughts that once I had,
Better by far you should forget and smile
Than that you should remember and be sad.

Some poems have such a "loose" structure that early critics denounced such productions as not even being poems. Carl Sandburg's poem entitled *Grass* was particularly criticized for its lack of rhyme, its irregular rhythm, and the prose insert in lines 7–9, but these lines carry a powerful impact, because it suggests that most people are completely unaware of some of the great tragic battles in modern history.

Grass

Pile the bodies high at Austerlitz and Waterloo.
Shovel them under and let me work —
    I am grass; I cover all.

And pile them high at Gettysberg
And pile them high at Ypres and Verdun.
Shovel them under and let me work.
Two years, ten years, and passengers ask the conductor:
    What place is this?
    Where are we now?

> I am grass.
> Let me work.

The translation of highly structured literary productions is always a problem because the very process of translation seems to require a rather high degree of parallelism in both form and content. Ezra Pound's translations of Chinese poetry were more like musical "variations on a theme" rather than actual translations, but Pound's artistry with words produced results that attracted considerable praise. But some poetry simply defies close or even loose translation. One professional translator of Japanese literature into English was asked to translate all of the poems of a noted Japanese poet, but he refused. He did, however, offer to translate all the poems that could be poems in English, because he recognized that many of the cultural allusions could not be satisfactorily translated into English, and introducing extensive notes about cultural differences would destroy the remarkable poetic character of the original poems.

Essentially the same problems exist in translating some Arabic and Chinese poems into English. Translators of poetry from Arabic into English have been conspicuously more successful than translators of poetry from Chinese into English, perhaps because the poems in Arabic have seemed to be closer to the Western World as the result of centuries of culture contact. But some translators of Chinese texts into English have felt constrained to communicate something of their distinctive cultural heritage by means of translated poetry, and as a result many translations of Chinese poetry have been much less successful. Poetry is not the medium for communicating cultural distinctiveness, and recently there has been a marked shift in Chinese thought about such issues, due in considerable measure to the literary journal *Renditions*, published by the Chinese University of Hong Kong.

5.2 Major content features of texts

In addition to organizational features of time, space, class, etc., texts also have important features of content: completeness, unity, novelty, appropriateness, and relevance, which in various ways and in different proportions make texts effective.

Completeness normally means that a text appears to cover the entire subject suggested by the title or by the topic paragraph that defines the range of content. Readers appreciate an article that seems to cover a subject adequately. In some cases, however, a text seems to drag on too long, as at the end of Tolstoy's *War and Peace*.

In addition, however, there needs to be some sense of unity. The beginning and the end need to be somehow related. As already noted, even in the short paragraph about kreteks, the occurrence of *Indonesia* in the first and last sentence helps to provide this sense of unity.

If an author is going to hold the attention of readers, a text must also include something novel and unexpected. A short-story, and especially detective novels, must include events that are not anticipated by readers. If the end of a book is almost predictable from the beginning, it will soon be neglected by readers.

Texts also need to be appropriate for the setting in which they are communicated. A lecture and a sermon may have somewhat the same purpose, that is, to significantly influence the thought and behavior of listeners, but the contents of a lecture or of a sermon are based on quite different sources of information and respond to quite different sets of presuppositions. Lecturers normally cite important new discoveries, while preachers refer to divinely inspired ancient writings. Furthermore, the language registers for lectures and sermons are quite distinct. On one occasion, for example, a visiting preacher greeted different members of a congregation after the benediction, and a small boy said to the preacher, "That was sure a nice talk." The boy's mother immediately intervened and insisted, "That was a sermon, not a talk," but the boy replied, "It wasn't a sermon, because he made us all laugh."

Relevance for receptors of communication is a major factor in communication, but relevance depends on a number of factors: the intelligibility of the contents of a text, the extent to which a receptor thinks he or she can benefit from the contents, and the physical and psychological proximity between the receptor and the contents. A notice about the death of more than 10,000 persons drowned in a tidal wave and flood in Bangladesh may seem much less relevant than the armed robbery of a house next door, unless, of course, a family member happens to have been in Bangladesh at the time.

5.3 Rhetorical features of a text

In order to enhance the impact and appeal of a text, all languages employ a number of formal and semantic features. The number and distribution of such features differs widely in different kinds of texts and in different languages.

The principal formal features include unusual word order (placing the subject at the end rather than at the beginning of a sentence), repetition of words or phrases (for emphasis), embedding of one idea within another, the incorporation of parenthetical information (usually in parenthesis or set off by commas), measured lines (as a part of poetic structures), parallelism (widely employed in liturgical and political texts that frequently include responses between speaker and audience), a telegraphic style (e.g. Hemingway) in contrast with elaborate rhetorical structures (Faulkner), back-flashes and forward-flashes (information that is not in a normal temporal sequence), parallelism and chiasm (the order abcabc in contrast with abccba), rhyme (previously regarded as indispensable for poetry , but more recently considered somewhat pedantic and artificial), rhythm (either in terms of various types of feet: iambic, trochaic, spondee, anapest, and dactyl, based on stress contrasts, length of syllables, and even on tone patterns in Classical Chinese), highlighting (emphasizing some feature of the content by order of words or by the amount of information employed to characterize some entity), purposeful deletion (*if you do that, I'll...!* in which case the lack of a specific threat may be more forceful than an actual threat), ungrammatical arrangement of words to call special attention to certain aspects of a text (technically called, anacoloutha, for which E. E. Cummings was rightly famous). For example, note his following four-line poem:

since feeling is first
who pays any attention
to the syntax of things
will never wholly kiss you

Some of the more important semantic features of texts include plays on the meanings of words (puns), purposeful ambiguity or obscurity (especially in detective stories), irony and sarcasm, understating (litotes) and overstating (hyperbole), euphemisms (using acceptable ways of speaking about something bad or taboo), specific reference in contrast with generic reference, indirection (saying one thing while actually referring to something else, for example, indicating the wealth of someone by saying that he has a ten room apartment on Park Avenue at 61st street in New York City), oxymorons as means of calling special attention to some entity or features (for example, *square circle, chaotic silence*), figurative language (for example, Sandburg's use of *throwing confetti and blowing horns* to characterize life and *in the dust...in the cool tombs* to describe death).

Many people associate figurative language almost exclusively with literary texts, especially poetry and novels, but scientists often need figurative expressions to explain some of the remarkable aspects of science. Note the following statements from the introduction to *The Lives of a Cell* by Lewis Thomas: "Evolution is still an infinitely long and tedious biological game, with only the winners staying at the table, but the rules are beginning to look more flexible. We live in a dancing matrix of viruses that dart rather like bees, from organism to organism, from plant to insect to mammal to me and back again, and into the sea, tugging along pieces of this genome, strings of genes from that, transplanted grafts of DNA, passing around heredity as though at a great party."

The following figurative uses of language are taken from a series of articles in *Science News* (July 3, 1999), but they represent only a few of the relatively wide range of semantic "oddities."

1.   In an article about the discovery of sharpened stone points found in the neck bone of a wild ass that died some 50,000 years ago, the discovery is called *an archeological smoking gun* since the manufacture of such weapons by Neanderthals has been generally denied.

In this same article a key paragraph ends with the statement *stone points added a deadly edge.* The name of the article also contains an interesting semantic shift: *Neanderthal Hunters Get to the Point.*

2.   An article on the ways in which malaria disrupts the immune system speaks about the T-cells as the *workhorses* of the immune system and insists that *dendrite cells, as an area of investigation, are hot right now.*

3.   An article entitled *Outta sight! A crafty peek at the sun's back* is about studies of the far side of the sun. The first sentence ends with the statement *astronomers are no longer in the dark,* since they can pick up the location of an ultraviolet hot spot by equipment in the Solar and Heliospheric Observatory.

4.   An article entitled *Amino acid puts the muscle in mussel glue* about the unusually strong adhesive used by mussels to attach themselves to wave lashed rocks describes the cross-linking protein strands that have *to kick in in order for the adhesive to perform.*

5.   An article entitled *If Mom chooses Dad, more ducklings survive* presents evidence that a female mallard duck that gets to pick her mate has ducklings that are more likely to survive. The researcher is herself surprised at the results, which are summarized in the statement, *The mothers build the nest, the mothers sit on the nest, the kids feed themselves, but the daddies hang around. We don't get it.*

6.   The article on the manner in which the DNA of some bacterias are transformed into crystals when a food source is strictly limited is highlighted by a clever parody, *when the going gets tough, the tough stop growing.*

7. An important article entitled *Stop-and Go Science* about the problems of traffic in cities around the world describes how scientists are trying very hard *to cram more vehicles onto existing roadways without putting highway speeds into a nose-dive.* But the number of theories about traffic flow include *a whole zoo of models.* No one, however, seems to understand how cars suddenly slow down to the same speed and *jell into a type of unified, moving mass.*

8. A fascinating article about the extent of carbon-dioxide in the environment during the last 10,000 years *is threatening to upend ideas about how much of this greenhouse gas filled the atmosphere before the industrial revolution.* But the study of carbon-dioxide in birch leaves from an ancient Dutch bog *gets a chilly reception from ice-core researchers.*

9. An article about *the Secret Lives of Squirrel Monkeys* describes a male Pacino monkey in Surinam as an animal who *brawls hard and dirty, and he stoically takes his licks. Constant no-holds-barred battles have left wicked scars on his mouth and nose...the undisputed champ of daily tooth-and-claw clashes* But the social arrangements of Pacino and his terrorized troop in Surinam are as different from those of Costa Rican squirrel monkeys *as the street gang's code of conduct is from Amish etiquette. Moreover, Peruvian squirrel monkeys take another path altogether, emphasizing what some might call "girl power."*

None of the above underlined expressions is particularly obscure in meaning for a person who has a reasonable command of English, but the extent to which such figurative expressions can be translated directly into another language depends on the creativity of the translator and on the presumed knowledge of the intended readers. Most readers are likely to know a "street gang's code of conduct," but they may not know anything about "Amish etiquette," and a footnote about the Amish people might seem overdone, although it might be useful to employ in the text "the behavior of those who refuse to employ force to defend their rights." Here is precisely where the knowledge and judgment of translators are crucial, and this is precisely why exceptional translators produce unusually good translations.

Working out a set of rules for adapting figurative expressions from one language to another is usually a waste of time because no two situations are ever really the same. The purposes of a publication, the intended audience, the ways in which a text will be used, and the special skills and knowledge of the translator are all factors that vary radically from one text to another. But in order to become more sensitive to what professional translators actually do, it is essential to study translations by expert translators. This can perhaps be best done by

asking three fundamental questions concerning additions, deletions, and changes in form and meaning.
1. What are the specific differences between the source and receptor texts? 2. What are the apparent contextual reasons for such differences? 3. What sociolinguistic factors seem to justify or question such differences?

In order to indicate more precisely what is involved in studying texts and their translation an illustrative paragraph has been selected from a bilingual publication in French and English, published for air travelers by Air France. The title of the article is "Spielberg, the Phoenix of Hollywood" by François Forestier, October, 1998 (the translator is, however, not named). But in order to examine a number of features of the translation, the various differences are indicated by corresponding numbers in square brackets preceding the corresponding expressions.

French text:
[1] Pour 139 dollars par semaine, Spielberg [2] loue alors un deux-pièces à Los Angeles. [3] Très rapidement, [4] il se voit confier la réalisation d'épisodes télé: il tourne *Eyes* avec Joan Crawford. La star, [5] réalisant que le jeune cinéaste n'a aucune expérience, [6] pique une colère. [7] Spielberg tient bon. [8] On lui confie un épisode de *Colombo*, et deux ou trois autres petits jobs. En 1972, il se lance dans un long métrage [9] bizarre, un truc intitulé *Duel*, [10] qui dure 74 minutes. [11] L'odyssée d'un conducteur poursuivi par un camion anonyme, sans raison apparente. [12] Le patron de la chaîne de télé NBC voit le film, demande: [13] "Qu'est-ce que c'est que ça? [14] et laisse faire." Spielberg en profite pour présenter le film dans des festivals, dont celui d'Avoriaz. Un an plus tard, [15] *Duel* sort sur les écrans, [16] rallongé à 85 minutes. C'est la sensation. [17] Tourné pour quelques dizaine de milliers de dollars, le film décuple la mise. [18] "J'ai décidé de passer au cinéma," déclare alors Spielberg. Il a vingt-quatre ans.

English translation:
Spielberg [2] rented a two-room, [1] $139-a-week apartment in Los Angeles. [3] He [4] was asked to direct episodes for TV series and made *Eyes* with Joan Crawford. The star [6] flew off the handle [5] when she found out that the young man didn't have any experience, [7] but Spielberg stood his ground. [8] He was asked to do an episode of *Colombo* as well as two or three other small jobs. In 1972 he made his first full-length feature, [9] a bizarre thriller called *Duel*. [10] Seventy-four minutes [11] about a faceless, psychopathic truck driver who tries to run a motorist off a California highway for no apparent reason. [12] When the head of NBC saw the movie he asked, [13] "What the hell is that?" [14] but gave it his seal of approval. Spielberg took advantage by pre-

senting *Duel* at several festivals, including Avoriaz. One year later [15,16] an eighty-five minute version hit the screens. It was a sensation. [17] The film, which cost only a few tens of thousands of dollars to make, paid back its investment tenfold. [18] "That's when I decided to leave TV for the movies," Spielberg says. He was twenty-four.

The English translator of the French text is exceptionally qualified in matching the journalistic style of the French text, particularly in the appropriate correspondences in idiomatic words and phrases, many of which are not mentioned in the following notes. From the various modifications and additions made in the translation, it is evident that the translator is much more knowledgeable about the motion picture industry than the writer. But the following analysis of the similarities and differences does not include all of the minor details nor every time some such feature recurs, for example, the use of different English tense forms for the journalistic present tense in French.

1.   The English text begins typically with the personal subject, rather than with an adverbial phrase.

2.   The French text employs primarily present-tense forms, but these are generally recast into appropriate past tense expressions in English.

3.   The French text says nothing at this point about the speed with which Spielberg progressed in the motion picture industry, but there are numerous references to this in other parts of the French article, and apparently the translator believed that this would also be an appropriate place to repeat this theme.

4.   The French text has a complex reflexive verb phrase with *voir* "to see," that functions like a passive, and accordingly, the English text employs *was asked.*

5.   The participial phrase construction between the subject and the main verb is typical in French, but unusual in English. In fact, a literal translation would have made the English text sound more like a legal document. Accordingly, the English text moves directly from the subject to the idiom expressing anger, and the cause of the anger occurs in the predicate of the English translation.

6.   The French idiom *pique une colère* literally, "sting an anger" is appropriately rendered in English as "flew off the handle," although the translator could have used a number of different expressions, "got angry," "became furious," "showed her temper."

7.   The French idiom *tient bon*, literally, "to hold well," is a common expression for "standing firm" or "refusing to yield" or "refusing to give in."

8.   The French phrase with an impersonal subject, the dative pronoun, and

the verb *confier* is somewhat more formal than the English translation, but the English passive *was asked* is a typical way of representing the impersonal French expression.

9.   In the French text the term *bizarre* qualifies the noun *métrage*, a French equivalent of a full-length feature. But in English the adjective *bizarre* goes much better with the following term *truc*, a popular term for a thriller.

10.   The French text places the clause about "lasting 74 minutes" at the end of the sentence. But the English text breaks the text at this point and combines the phrase "Seventy-four minutes" with the following sentence. This change in sentence content makes a better transition and helps to explain somewhat the translator's unusual addition.

11.   Whereas the French text only speaks about "the trip of a driver pursued by a nameless truck without reason," the translator evidently felt that such a description of the motion picture did not do justice to a film that had such an important impact on Spielberg's career. The statements in the two texts are not necessarily contradictory, but certainly the English text contains a substantive addition.

12.   In the French text the writer evidently thought that it was necessary to identify the NBC as a television company, but to the translator such an addition apparently seemed unnecessary. In the French text the two parts represent structurally two different sentences, although semantically they are logically related. According, the English translator made this connection evident by translating, *When the head of NBC saw the movie, he asked,*

13.   Although the French text has only the literal statement, "*What's that!*" the context certainly suggests something more surprising and unusual. The English translator evidently felt it was important to translate in terms of the context, not merely in terms of the words.

14.   The French text has only a phrase meaning literally "and let it be done," but the context suggests much more. In the case of expressions marked as 13 and 14, the English translator has evidently tried to make the text more realistic by translating what was evidently implied by what was said.

15, 16.   These two segments of the French text and the English translation need to be treated together because of a complex problem of order. In the French text the expression *Duel sort sur les écrans* is a perfectly natural ways of talking by releasing a film to theater chains. But in view of the fact that the picture proved to be a sensation, it apparently seemed to the translator that something like "hit the screens" would be more appropriate.

In the French text the statement *rallongé à 85 minutes*, literally "lengthened to 85 minutes" would perhaps depreciate the value of what was added. Accordingly, the English translation has simply *an eighty-five minute version.*

17. In French the participial phrase that precedes the main part of the sentence is typical in French (in fact, such constructions were also popular with Cicero in ancient Rome). But a literal translation into English would be particularly awkward. It is for this reason, that the English translation begins with the subject and is then followed by a restrictive clause.

18. The French text means only "passing to motion pictures" or "changing to motion pictures," but the English translator evidently believed that it was important to indicate that Spielberg was giving up work on television shows and would be working completely for the movies. This is simply an edition to make the text more explicit and clear.

This type of study of what expert professional translators actually do is the best way to learn how to translate. Such an approach is far better than attempting to memorize rules about embedded clauses, figurative meanings, and stylistic equivalences. A translator needs to develop a "feeling" for what is appropriate for different types of texts being translated for different kinds of audiences who will no doubt use the translation for different purposes. What translators need most of all is judgment, and this can only be acquired by seeing what competent translators have done and by experimenting with different kinds of texts for different types of audiences. Personal guidance by competent teachers is far better than any textbook on translating, because translating is essentially a skill, and skills are best learned in an apprenticeship context. This, however, also means that teachers of translation need to be expert translators.

CHAPTER 6

Representative treatments of translating

The basic principles of translating are not as diverse or as intricate as many persons think. In most instances their apparent differences largely reflect different kinds of content, diverse audiences, and distinct purposes. Accordingly, it may be useful to look more carefully at various books on translation, especially because the practice of translating and interpreting in the 20th Century has increased much more rapidly than at any other time in history. The expansion of world trade, the development of multinational corporations and international entities, such as the United Nations, NATO, the European Union, and regional groupings in Southeast Asia and Africa, inevitably increase the need for translation and interpretation.

The need for such cooperative efforts is highlighted by the fact that populations are rapidly outgrowing natural resources, especially water, and some irresponsible dictators still rattle atomic weapons. But fortunately, our electronic age now makes possible interlingual communication on a level never dreamed of before. Email and internet are making the world a multi-language community.

6.1 Developments in interlingual studies

In order to match the need for interlingual communication, the teaching of foreign languages is rapidly increasing, and in Europe alone there are at least seventy-five institutions concentrating on teaching the principles and practice of translating and interpreting. In addition, many university departments of foreign languages are introducing courses in interlingual communication.

There are now more than forty academic journals dealing with the issues of translation and interpreting, and during the 20th Century more than 300 books have been published about problems and solutions to interlingual communication. The number of professional translators has grown enormously. In the European Union there are some 2,500 in-house translators, while in Hong Kong alone there are some 6,000 full-time free-lance and agency translators. The Professional Translators Society of China has a membership of more than

40,000 translators, and the total number of people in the world spending either most or all of their time translating or interpreting probably exceeds 300,000, but they cannot keep up with the demand.

A number of commercial firms are also investing heavily in programs for translating. Already there are more than eighty-five sets of languages for which there is at least some automated system for translating, and there are more than 400 orthographic systems for computer use. Internet translating and interpreting represents a thirty billion dollar a year market that is growing at the rate of 14% percent a year.

In a number of academic institutions translating and interpreting have evidently become academic disciplines in their own right, especially if one regards the development of technical vocabulary as an index of professional status. Consider, for example, the following representative English terms employed in speaking and writing about translating and interpreting: *conceptual paradigms, polysystems, skopos, poststructuralism, computerized corpora, postcolonialization, globalization, subspecialties, cultural studies, literary theory, culturally oriented research, competing paradigms, conceptual and disciplinary divisions, abstract category of verbal communication, minimal processing effort, Hallidayan linguistic theory, interpersonal pragmatics, audiovisual synchronization, systematic loss of politeness phenomena, computerized corpora, explicitation hypothesis, sanitization, computer-discovered regularities in translation strategies, poststructuralist translation theory, discursive self-definition, confrontation with alien discourses, transdiscursive texts, the rhetoricity of language, gendering, Gricean mechanism.* If specialized vocabulary is a sign of a separate, emerging discipline, there is no doubt that translating and interpreting are creating a good deal of academic autonomy, static, and status.

Professional specialization has become so extensive that some people insist on separating translating and interpreting into two distinct disciplines of interlingual communication. As already noted, interpreters need considerably greater immediate knowledge about the subject matter being communicated, and they must also make more rapid decisions and be less nervous about their own limitations. But interpreters and translators deal with essentially the same problems of textual correspondences.

One important reason for skepticism about the need for more books on translation is that some people seem to have a special gift for interlingual communication, and without any formal training in translating they become first-rate translators. They appear to have an exceptional aptitude for effective interlingual communication, and they simply do not need years of training. In fact, it is often said that particularly competent translators and interpreters are born, not made.

More and more evidence seems to point to the fact that highly creative translating and interpreting are largely inherent skills similar to what occurs in the fields of music and graphic art. Almost anyone can learn to draw pictures of a landscape or play music in an amateurish way, but people must have unusual innate aptitudes if they are to be professionally successful.

Perhaps the description of the training and experience of two real persons, purposely named Marcos and Guillaume respectively so as not to reveal their true identity, may be helpful in understanding the nature of interlingual skill in communication.

Marcos grew up in a strictly monolingual context of Spanish, but he had the advantage of an excellent education in Latin and Greek and went on to learn French, German, and English, although he never learned to speak German or English because he had no opportunity to live in countries where these languages were spoken. As a part of his teaching Classical Greek and Latin, he did a considerable amount of translating, and a number of his translations of Latin and Greek authors, as well as books translated from French, German, and English, were published in Spanish. In fact, he ultimately wrote several books on the history and practice of translating and was honored by his academic colleagues for unusual competence in translating.

By way of contrast, Guillaume was educated in a trilingual setting of German, French, and English, and spoke all three languages without noticeable accent. His university training was exceptional and because of his language competence he became a translator in companies in the United States doing business with affiliates in Europe. Because of extensive experience as a trilingual translator, he was hired by a New York firm to handle all translations of documents and correspondence involving English, French, and German.

His translations were not regularly reviewed, but gradually responses from affiliates in Europe indicated that they had evidently not accurately understood the translations in German and French. In fact, after a few months one affiliate wrote confidentially to say that it would be much more satisfactory if communications could be sent in English, because people in Europe were confused and were wasting too much time trying to figure out the meaning of letters and documents in French and German.

Guillaume had no psychological blocks in speaking foreign languages, because he spoke them freely, but he had evidently not understood that translating means correct communicating, and as a result his word-for-word written renderings were often misleading. In fact, it seems incredible that a competent trilingual speaker could so seriously misunderstand the nature of translating. Some people, however, seem to never overcome the serious mistake of thinking that translating means representing consistently the dictionary meaning of words. His speech never betrayed such word-for-word correspondences, but in translating he was intellectually blind to the nature of his task as a translator.

Skill in translating is not a common commodity. For example, from time to time the European Union sends out a notice about an examination for people wanting to be in-house translators of the EU. Frequently, more than 15,000 persons will apply, but the total number of persons who are permitted to take the examination is greatly reduced on the basis of language experience and academic training. As a result a typical number of persons actually taking an examination is approximately 5,000, but the number that are successful in passing the examination is normally less than ten. As already noted in Chapter 1, the aptitude for special competence in interlingual communication is about as restricted as it is for music and art.

Competence in translating and interpreting may be meaningfully discussed in terms of the position of people on a bell-curve with the typical two dimensions: the horizontal dimension indicating the degree of competence from practically no ability to extremely creative ability and the vertical dimension indicating the approximate number of persons at each point along the curve. Such curves are useful devices for grasping certain important concepts, even when it is impossible to assign numerical values to the numbers of persons and the degrees of competence.

Persons on the left of such a curve will generally be inadequate for effective translating, and up to a point near the top of the curve most people should probably not be encouraged to become professional translators or interpreters, although they may be good mathematicians, expert clothing designers, or first-rate administrators. At the same time, it is essential to recognize the importance of motivation in all such situations, because high motivation can compensate to some extent for lack of inherent ability.

Those with competence near the top of the curve and down the major part of the right hand side of the curve can certainly learn to translate various types of largely routine documents, such as letters, newspaper articles, business agendas, political speeches, and government notices. These are precisely the persons who can benefit significantly from courses in translating offered by universities and institutes with intensive programs lasting three or four years. But for texts with considerable figurative language, legal terminology, merchandizing, and scientific content, it is important to have persons who are especially competent in understanding the source text and in reproducing the content and the style in another language. Even some of the most gifted translators can and do profit from a study of what other first-rate translators actually do. Such realistic studies of translation principles and practice can greatly enrich their own work.

The description and classification of texts on the basis of form and content, and therefore of interpretation, may be useful in speaking about types of translation problems. For the most part, it is possible to characterize five different, but somewhat overlapping, types of texts, although some of the following text types may have overlapping features:

1.   Texts in which the words, grammar, and discourse structure represent the ordinary day-to-day experience found in personal letters, news reports, agendas, commercial advertising, business notices, daily progress reports, and many short stories. Such texts generally contain well known words and except for common idioms, they employ few figurative expressions.

2.   Texts with relatively well-known words (although often with highly specific meanings) and complex grammar so as to include a number of restrictive features within sentence units, for example, laws, constitutions, bylaws, wills, and contracts.

3.   Texts with highly technical vocabulary having very specific meanings and relatively clear grammatical constructions, for example, books on science, technical journals, instructions for engaging in scientific processes.

4. Texts with unusual figurative meanings of words, for example, cult histories, elaborate mantras, translations of the Koran and the Bible, and memorized texts of secret societies.

5.   Texts with numerous idiomatic expressions and types of content that require figurative interpretation, for example, myths, parables, proverbs, lyric poetry, songs, operas, and symbolic novels

To this list of five basic text types, it may be useful to mention another important, but highly restricted text type, namely, political documents prepared for international bodies about rapidly developing events. Such documents must be factually true, or the leaders will be severely criticized. Nevertheless, these documents usually cannot tell all the truth, since reference to or even indirect allusions to such matters could serious damage future developments. Political leaders and their speech writers, as well as their translators, must be sensitive to both the content of reports and the possible emotive responses of audiences. As a result, some political leaders feel constrained to talk but to say little or nothing, and translators are under great pressure to do the same.

Translators and interpreters must also be constantly aware of different types of audiences: school children, sports fans, retirees, and professionals with their own jargons. They must also be aware that texts may have different purposes. Some are simply for amusement and enjoyment while others are crucial for what people want to do, for example, how to assemble a complicated machine

Many translators enjoy the challenge of literary texts, even those that are almost on the margin of intelligibility, for example, the highly figurative writing of James Joyce. Others like the complexity of Faulkner's sentences, and they may even believe that a strictly word-for-word translation communicates certain hidden concepts that freer translations overlook. For example, Buber and Rosenzweig made a literal translation of the Hebrew Bible so as to give German readers a "feeling" of how ancient Hebrew speakers might have understood the text. Chouraqui has attempted to do this in French, and a comparable word-for-word translation of Genesis 1.1–2 into English would be: "Heading, Elohim was creating the heavens and the earth, the earth was tohu-bohu, darkness was on the faces of the abyss, but the breath of Elohim spread out over the faces of the water."

Other translators find the greatest challenge in the intellectual task of communicating significant information so as to produce important responses in the activity and beliefs of people in other language-cultures. Their concern is for the ways in which receptors understand, appreciate, and respond to a translation. They regard translating and interpreting as communication, and what counts for them is the correctness with which the messages are received.

6.2 Illustrative examples of different treatments of translating

The generally negative reaction of students to books about principles of translating are due in part to fact that they have not had enough practice in translating to be able to evaluate or criticize such books in a relevant manner. In addition, many of the textbooks appear to use a vocabulary designed to impress educators that translation is a legitimate academic discipline. But what puzzles students most is that the various books are really not that different. They all seem to be saying much the same things but with different illustrative data, diverse technical vocabulary, and prescriptive advice without explanations of the empirical sources of such principles

Because of the reaction of many students who bring up such issues during discussion periods following lectures, it may perhaps be useful to characterize briefly some of the more insightful books. But I have included primarily those books that state principles of translation and follow these up with plenty of useful examples. Some of these volumes are, however, pedagogical textbooks designed to teach students step by step how to translate various kinds of texts. The order of presentation of these volumes is based on dates of publication.

1. *Zielsprache* by Fritz Guttinger (1963) is a delightfully written book that begins with the controversial and negative statements by Ortega y Gasset, Goethe, Schleiermacher, and Benjamin, but ends with a fascinating collection of some of the most important statements about translation in the 19th and early 20th Century. The titles of the chapters indicate quite clearly the down-to-earth character of the volume: "Translating (more or less) literary texts," "Everything that is useful for a translator," "Five sources for making mistakes," and "When translating is the same as writing." The range of problems dealt with is excellent, and although the text is in German, most of the illustrative examples are from English.

2. *Toward a Science of Translating* by Eugene A. Nida (1964) attempts to apply to translating the relevant insights from linguistics, sociolinguistics, sociosemiotics, cultural anthropology, lexicology, and communication theory. The principal source of illustrative data is Bible translations, and the prospective audience was the several thousand persons engaged in translating the Scriptures into more than a 1,000 languages.

Unfortunately many people assumed that my concepts of translation developed as a result of working on biblical texts, but my ideas about translating were formulated years earlier while a Greek Major at the University of California at Los Angeles. I was introduced to the writings of such persons as Sapir, Bloomfield, Pedersen, and Malinowski. I therefore saw no reason why the everyday Koine Greek of the New Testament should not be translated into the everyday level of languages spoken throughout the world.

The volume *Toward a Science of Translation* reflects a number of different insights from diverse disciplines because no single discipline or theory can possibly provide the necessary insights to deal satisfactorily with the many faceted aspects of interlingual communication.

3. *Introducción a la Traductología* by Gerardo Vázquez-Ayora (1977), with a subtitle of *Basic Course in Translating*, is a systematic course for translating from English into Spanish based on linguistic principles and divided into nine principal chapters: Preliminary analysis of a text, The application of linguistics to trans-

lating, Style, Frequent syntactic and lexical differences between English and Spanish, The application of linguistics and metalinguistics to ambiguity and redundancy, Discourse, Technical procedures in translating, and General procedures in translation — all with consistent attention to equivalence and context.

The section on style deals extensively with optional and obligatory distinctions, and the treatment of anglicisms is unusually extensive. Most of the longer texts, however, come largely from literary sources. References to the views of other specialists in translation are extensive and well documented, and the sections on translation procedures are often quite practical, but the technical terminology used to explain translation principles is translated literally from English in such a way as to profoundly disturb Spanish speakers, who generally dislike technical terms that are not properly formed on traditional models. Nevertheless, Georgetown University Press is to be congratulated for publishing a book that has been so helpful to many Latin Americans.

4.   *Traduire: théorèmes pour la traduction,* by J-R Ladmiral (1979) deals with a number of basic translation issues from a psychological perspective. The first chapter "What is translation?" is a rapid review of developments in the field of interlingual communication. The second chapter on translation and teaching programs deals with a wide range of issues: from the correct understanding of the source text to the sociological implications of translating. The third chapter also considers a broad series of issues, from the philosophy of language to the nature of literature. The fourth chapter treats issues of stylistics, connotations, sociolinguistic problems, and the various ways in which translations may be effectively critiqued. Chapter five is a particularly effective analysis of semantics and semiotics, and a final Chapter 6 analyzes the practical application of basic translation principles. The Appendix also continues an insightful analysis of psychoanalytical discourse. The range of Ladmiral's interests and competence thoroughly justifies his criticisms of polemical, historical, and theoretical arguments against translating. While his interesting, clear style of writing makes this important book a real pleasure to read, his profound knowledge and insight about translating makes a reader see translation in a much broader frame of reference.

5.   *The Science of Linguistics in the Art of Translation* by Joseph L. Malone (1988) has a very useful section on technical vocabulary about linguistic factors in translating and departs from most other analyses of translation by introducing dialogue as a fundamental factor in translating. The book is divided into three parts, with several chapters in each part. Part One deals with equation and substitution, divergence and convergence, amplification and reduction,

repackaging, reordering, and trajection, while Part Two is concerned primarily with systematic and formalistic techniques, taxonomies, syntactic representations, and bridge techniques. Part Three treats phonetics, phonology and poetic form, rhyme, alliteration, paranomasia, and parallax.

Although the technical vocabulary may seem somewhat overwhelming, the consistency with which the terms are used and the relevance of the related concepts are so important that a reader soon appreciates the important underlying distinctions. There is also a very useful range of different types of texts and languages, for example, English, French, German, Latin, Irish, Yiddish, Norwegian, Japanese, Greek, Hebrew, Accadian, Chinese, Bengali, Russia, and Spanish. This is not a book for beginners, but it can be of great help for people with a good linguistic background, because it explores in a systematic manner some of the most common problems of translating. Chapter 10 on zeroes is especially important since the absence of correspondence is so consistently overlooked by many teachers of translation. The Bibliography and the Index of Persons and Translation Resources are unusually valuable.

6.   *Translation Studies, an Integrated Approach* by Mary Snell-Hornby (1988) is an excellent short book for any translator or teacher of translation. Chapter 1 treats translation studies as an independent discipline, and Chapter 2 focuses on translation as a cross-cultural event. Chapter 3 analyzes translation from various orientations, for example, linguistics, text analysis, speech acts, the dynamics of meaning, and interlingual relations. Chapter 4 treats translation from the wide range of "special languages" to literary translation.

This small book of only 163 pages contains an amazing amount of significant information about the principles and practice of translating, written in down-to-earth language about a wide range of constantly recurring issues. The diagram on page 89, representing the translational equivalents on page 88, is an especially effective way for dealing with types of speech acts, participant status, grammatical structure, and vocabulary. Other diagrammatic representations of this type could do a great deal to provide structured ways of imaging the relevance of various linguistic structures.

7.   *Discourse and the Translator* by Basil Hatim and Ian Mason (1990) is an excellent treatment of eleven topics that are crucial to the theory and practice of translating: issues and debates about translation studies, important relations between theory and practice, the role of context in translating, the significance of discourse, the pragmatics of context, the semiotic dimension of context, intertextuality and intentionality, text types as a focus for translators, text

structure. discourse texture, and the translator as a mediator.

The linguistic orientation of this volume is Hallidayan functional linguistics with special emphasis on socio-cultural contexts. The authors make an important distinction between actual and virtual problems of translation and explain the lack of interest in linguistics by professional translators as the result of undue emphasis on formal structures rather than on meaningful relations. Language variation in the form of registers and dialects plays a major role, but the principal issues relate to the nature and role of discourses in a broad semiotic sense.

8.   *Translation and Relevance* by Ernst-August Gutt (1991) is an application of relevance theory to the issues of interlingual interpretation of texts, first, in terms of style, as ways in which thoughts are expressed, and second, the related communicative clues consisting of semantic representations, syntactic properties, phonetic features, semantic constraints, formulaic expressions, ono-matopoeia, the stylistic value of words, and the sound-based poetic features.

Gutt focuses primarily on the inferential nature of communication, that is, the mental faculty that enables people to communicate with one another by drawing inferences from all kinds of human behavior.

Gutt's concern is not so much with the details of interlingual communication but with offering a different approach to tricky problems. A valid definition of translation in the relevance-theoretic framework is given as "A receptor language utterance is a direct translation of a source language utterance if and only if it purposes to interpretively resemble the original completely in the context envisaged for the original," but a number of words in this definition also require further refinement and specification. This volume does not attempt to illustrate the broad range of difficulties faced by translators, but Gutt has made an important contribution to translation studies by pointing out a different theoretical approach to the issue of communicative resemblance.

9.   *In Other Words* by Mona Baker (1992) is exactly what its subtitle indicates, namely, "a course-book on translation." The titles of the major chapters indicate quite clearly the linguistic Hallidayan approach to different levels and types of structures and texts: equivalence at word level, equivalence above the word level, grammatical equivalence, textual equivalence (thematic and information structures), textual equivalence, and pragmatic equivalence.

This volume is particularly appropriate for students beginning to study the problems of translating. The terminology is carefully explained and consistently used to describe translators' difficulties (there is also an excellent glossary). Many differences between languages such as English, German, Italian, and

Russian are carefully noted, and distinctions between various levels of English are consistently illustrated. Semantic fields and lexical sets are explained and their relevance to translation is repeatedly indicated in a consistent manner.

The introduction of numerous translational differences between English and Arabic (the author's mother tongue) is an important plus. And suggestions for further reading occur at the end of each chapter. Mona Baker is both a linguist and a teacher.

10. *Les Fondements Socio-Linguistiques de la Traduction* by Maurice Pergnier (1993) is a delightfully written book that serves to bring the first edition of 1978 up to date. The excellent range of topics includes chapters on the general theory of language, variables in language and speech, parameters of a text, translation between languages in contact, sense and signification, linguistic and sociolinguistic points of view, idioms as sociolinguistic features, analysis and exegesis, and translation and language universals, followed by a section on conclusions and perspectives. A final annex deals with mirages and realities of certain traditional concepts that may be used to measure methods and translational equivalences (the annex is well worth the price of the book)

The French language makes it possible for Pergnier to make some important terminological distinctions, for example, between *language, langue* and *parole* as well as between *signe, signifié* and *signification*. Translation is recognized as essentially a branch of semiotics, and accordingly, translators must recognize that discourses always have more than one possible meaning. But in order to determine a possible meaning, it is essential to understand the contexts of both encoding and decoding. Although the basic theoretical distinctions are sociolinguistic and sociosemiotic, the working terminology and orientation represent essentially Saussure's basic insights.

Some of the explanations of special translation problems may seem somewhat lengthy and even overdone, but the elegance of the style and the clarity of analysis are so convincing that a reader finds the explanations to be windows for learning rather than dark academic corridors leading nowhere. Pergnier is a genius in taking a simple English statement such as *I go to school* as a means of pointing out how the context can produce several different meanings. Pergnier always distinguishes clearly between a text as a discourse and a text as a message.

This volume is not a textbook for classes in translating, but rather, a source of brilliant insight about the nature of language and meaning.

11. *Traducción: Historia y Teoría* by Valentín García Yebra (1994) is an unusual book by an unusual person. The first part describes in an effective way the his-

tory of translation beginning with the early Sumerians, Accadians, Hittites, Ugarites, and Egyptians and mentions especially the legend of Gilgamesh that shows up in various forms in different languages, including Hebrew. The translation of Greek literature in the education of the Romans is clearly described, but especially important is the history of translation of Greek texts into Arabic, and their later translation from Arabic into Latin for people in Western Europe.

Translations made in Spain are divided into three epochs: the reign of Juan II, the Golden age of early Spanish literature, and translations made toward the end of the 20th Century, including especially the experience of Pierre Daniel Huet and of Yebra himself, who is not only a first rate translator of Greek, Latin, German, English and French, but a prolific writer and editor. The section on theory and criticism deals with the basic concepts that must guide all translators, but especially those translating into and from other romance languages, such as French, Italian, Spanish, and Portuguese. The last two sections on the variety of texts and translations and on the critical analysis of translation theories are particularly important, but the most interesting chapter describes Yebra's personal experience as a translator.

12. *Basic Concepts and Models for Interpreter and Translator Training* by Daniel Gile (1995) is particularly important in that it combines translating and interpreting as intimately related means for interlingual communication. Six chapters deal with both translation and interpretation but focus on various related factors: the theoretical components in training, communication and quality, fidelity, comprehension, knowledge acquisition, and literature on training. One chapter analyzes a sequential model of translation, while three chapters deal specifically with certain features of interpreting: the effort model of interpretation, coping tactics in interpretation, and language issues in conference interpreting, which in many respects also applies to translating.

On the issue of whether translators are born, rather than made, Gile rightly insists that formal training is not mandatory but it can help individuals to fully realize their potantial, something that no one would seriously dispute. Gile also sees great practical advantages in theoretical concepts and models, and applies these aspects of translation and interpreting to issues of professional loyalty (a subject that few books treat in a serious manner), because interpreters often serve purposes that are strictly marginal or even contradictory to their personal attitudes and roles.

Gile also pays a great deal of attention to full comprehension because translators and interpreters not only need to understand the language, but in many instances must have specialized knowledge about intricate relations between various forms of the same entity or state. The chapter on coping tactics for inter-pretation is especially useful since it clearly reflects actual practice, for example, delaying a response, reconstructing meaning from the context, getting help from someone else in the booth. But trying to read a script and interpret simul-taneously at the same time is extremely difficult, specially when speakers sud-denly depart from a script to emphasize some particularly important point.

13. *Descriptive Translation Studies and beyond* by Gideon Toury (1995) begins with an introduction in which Toury describes the basis for Descriptive Translation Studies. This first part consists of a thorough and convincing expo-sition of the need for descriptive studies, as proposed by some of the earlier cre-ative insights of Holmes. The following three parts are subdivided into twelve different chapters: that focus attention on such themes as the target culture, norms in translation, methods for descriptive studies, coupled pairs, an exem-plary study of descriptive studies, a Shakespearean sonnet, indirect translation, literary organization, interim solutions, the development of a translation (Hamlet's monologue in Hebrew), translation of specific lexical items, and experimentation in translation studies.

Some excursus are particularly interesting: 1. pseudo-translations, texts that pretend to be translations, but are not, for example, the portions of the Book of Mormon that come from the King James Bible, and similarly so-called original texts that are actually translations, and 2. the procedures involved in a bilingual person becoming a translator, a study of nature vs. nurture.

Part Four is particularly important in that Toury deals with the basic issue of "Laws of Translational Behavior" as probabilistic generalizations that consti-tute the foundation for his focus on Descriptive Translational Studies.

14. *Interpretation and Translation* by Elena Croitoru (1996) is designed pri-marily for Rumanians interested in present developments in translation stud-ies and in learning how to handle various forms of English for different pur-poses, for example, English for academic purposes, English for specific purpos-es, and English for science and technology. The text is divided into five princi-pal sections: 1. The interpretive processes required for effective translating, in which issues of text types, cultural input, and translational equivalence are pri-mary considerations, 2. Translating texts representing different types of English usage (especially English for Special Purposes), 3. Discourse analysis viewed from the perspectives of cohesion, coherence, texture, and contextual elements, 4. Difficulties encountered in dealing with texts employing English for science and technology (as a way of talking about text types), 5. Translation

competence in terms of communication strategies and different levels of competence in translating.

As in many practical situations language learning is combined with various aspects of translation since the learning of English is directly related to its use in translation. University programs in learning foreign languages can be justified more readily if the practical application to translating can be incorporated, even though theoretically and practically people should have a high level of language competence before they undertake to study translation principles and practices. This same problem, however, exists in a number of countries in Europe, Latin America, and Asia.

15. *Knowledge and Skills in Translator Behavior*, Wulfram Wilss (1996) is a wide-ranging treatment of eleven different aspects of translating: translation studies in terms of scope and challenges, theoretical and empirical aspects of translation studies, translation as knowledge-based activity, context, culture, compensation, translation as meaning-based information processing (including gradience, complexity, conventionality, schematicity, economy, and predictability), the translation process and translation procedures, the role of the translator in the translation process, discourse linguistics, decision making and choice, translation teaching, and human and machine translation.

In a text of only 232 pages Wilss has included an amazing range of problems and creative suggestions, including an incisive analysis of Chomsky's failures and the recognition of the creative implications of cognitive linguistics advocated so effectively by Langacker and others. Wilss' comments on text linguistics and translation form the core of his theoretical approach to language and translation, but his chapter on Context, Culture, and Compensation provides much of the substance that must go into the process of translating. Words and actions only have meaning in terms of linguistic and cultural contexts, and controlled compensations involve the basic adjustments required to communicate essentially the same source message in a target text.

16. *Manual de traducción, Inglés/Castellano* by Juan Gabriel López Guix and Jacqueline Minett Wilkinson (1997) contains ten chapters on the themes of the role of translators, the philosophy of language, the genius of language and its importance for translation, different syntactic features of English and Spanish, morphological differences in English and Spanish, differences of punctuation in English and Spanish, the significance of different theories of translation, different systems for analyzing texts, translation procedures, and dictionaries and other sources of help in translating. The chapter on the philosophy of language

cites almost all of the major contributors, including Bertrand Russel, Wittgenstein, Austin, Searle, Grice. Sapir, Whorf, Quine, Frege, and Coseriu. The chapter on grammar and universals seems to rely considerably on Chomsky, but the implications of transformations are largely abandoned.

The fourth and fifth chapters on differential features between English and Spanish are very well developed with a wide range of examples, and the eighth chapter on the analysis of texts is one of the most perceptive. Chapter nine concerning translation procedures is the core of the volume. This volume describes and illustrates numerous differences between Spanish and English on the basis of borrowings, traditional idioms, transpositions, modulation, equivalence, adaptation, expansion, reduction, and compensation. But as in many books on principles of translating, a reader obtains the impression that a translator translates languages, that is, develops a typology of linguistic contrasts as a means of understanding and reproducing the contents of texts. This, however, is a false concept of translating, which is not concerned with interpreting the structures of language but in reproducing the meaning of texts.

17. *My father taught me how to cry, but now I have forgotten: the semantics of religious concepts with an emphasis on meaning, interpretation, and translatability*, by Kjell Magne Yri (1998) does not appear to be a book about translation, but it is a very remarkable study of the meanings of two sets of words representing two of the most significant concepts in religion, namely, salvation and perdition. The long history of such words and the vicissitudes of diverse meanings in a lengthy historical series of translations points very clearly to the importance of cognitive linguistics (developed by Langacker, Lakoff, and Geeraerts) as a fundamental component of any scientific approach to semantics and translation.

As a missionary Bible translator of the Scriptures into the Sidaamo Afo, a Semitic language of Ethiopia, Yri was constantly confronted with the issues of the appropriateness of two sets of diametrically opposed concepts: (1) *save, savior, salvation*, and (2) *perish, destroy, be destroyed*, that exhibit a fascinating history in which innovation occurred repeatedly in the creative use of language by one individual after another. Accordingly, Yri rejects prototype semantics that depends on social phenomena. For Yri religious language is simply human language used to talk about religious matters. Yri also has some very important observations about expert and folk categories

Terms for *salvation* are studied first in their contexts of the Hebrew Bible, then in Classical Greek and in the Septuagint translation of the Hebrew Bible into Hellenistic Greek. The next stage is the use of these terms in the Greek New Testament, followed by developments in the Latin Vulgate, and for Yri's own background and that of other Norwegian missionaries in Ethiopia, namely, the rendering of these same concepts in Old Norse as well as in modern Norwegian. But the story must also include the special problems of correspondence in Sidaamu Afo, in which the metaphorical meaning of forgiveness is dominant.

The Hebrew words for *loss, perdition, destruction* are also traced through the long line of figurative meanings, and each stage of development is summarized by some excellent diagrams that indicate historical developments and degrees of semantic sameness by the thickness of lines enclosing different semantic domains. Yri also has some very valuable comments on the role of interpretation in translation, especially individual versus so-called objective meaning.

Yri contends that so-called "lexical meaning" is a linguistic illusion abstracted from communicative intension and interpretation. Accordingly, it is largely irrelevant to talk about the "same concept" in the source text and in the target text. The book ends with a definition of language in relation to translation: "language is the composite internal neural enterprise that enables one individual to communicate with another," to which he should probably have added "by means of oral sounds."

For beginning translators who would like to read some of the above books as a help to understanding more about translating, I would recommend starting with the following series, listed by authors and beginning with books that are likely to be more easily understood: Mary Snell-Hornby, Mona Baker, Valentin Garcia Yebra, and Daniel Gile.

Even a rapid glance at the above brief descriptions of various treatments of translating will soon reveal that despite considerable differences in vocabulary, the essential elements in translating and interpreting are very much the same, namely, an accurate understanding of the source text and an effective representation of the meaning in another language. Any one of the above statements of principles and procedures in interlingual communication can be the basis for satisfactory translating. And on the basis of such books a number of teachers have had real success in helping students to understand texts more thoroughly and to reproduce their meaning effectively.

In some of these discussions of the underlying principles and practices of translating, there is, however, a constantly recurring failure, namely, the treatment of translating as essentially a matter of translating languages rather than translating texts. No one says so specifically, but the implication is that translators need to have a broad understanding of the structures of the respective languages in order to understand what is happening in the processes of translating.

This intrusion of linguistics and sociolinguistics into the theory and practice of translating is the direct result of the fact that so many persons without an adequate knowledge of their A, B, and C languages want to learn how to translate. And in order to help such students, teachers have turned to linguistics, sociolinguistics, and even to sociosemiotics as a means of helping students understand some of the broader implications of what translating involves. As a result, teachers are required to teach languages and translating at the same time, when they ought to concentrate first on language learning by using the most modern and effective techniques and then on teaching translating, in which the focus can and should be on texts. Then translating becomes more and more like writing in one's own mother tongue. In fact, translating is nothing more than understanding correctly the meaning of a text and then reproducing this meaning in another language in such a manner that the stylistic features of the source text are adequately represented directly or indirectly.

I have great personal sympathy for teachers of translation who must try to do the impossible, namely, endeavor to teach translating to people who do not know the respective languages thoroughly. Unfortunately, most secondary and university programs do not teach languages, but teach about languages. For example, when I first visited Belgium some fifty years ago, I knew all the irregular forms of the French verb system, but I did not know how to exchange dollars for Belgian francs.

Instead of books that combine a study of linguistic structures and translating principles, what translators need most is a discovery procedure that will enable them to determine the meaning, the meanings, or the non-meaning of a text on the basis of relevant contexts. Such a procedure would concentrate attention on what concerns translators most directly and practically. Such a course would simply make explicit what expert translators constantly do in the process of translating.

Perhaps some of the following statements about becoming a translator may be of help:

a. Learning to translate

1. Acquire excellent competence in one or more foreign languages. Unfortunately many foreign language programs in universities focus on learning about languages rather than learning to understand and effectively speak and/or write such languages. Special language-learning programs, such as the Goethe Institutes, are expensive, and as a result students wishing to learn a language often apply to government sponsored programs teaching translating and interpreting. Ideally, most such institutes should dedicate the first two-thirds

of the program to intensive language learning and then introduce techniques of translating and interpreting for the final period, but educational authorities in some countries are still unaware of what can and should be done to improve foreign language efficiency.

2.   Analyze the meaning of a source text on the basis of concepts rather than the meanings of particular words because the concepts are the units that must form the basis for finding equivalent expressions in the receptor language. Since many documents are poorly written, it may be useful to rewrite certain portions of a text in order to ascertain more accurately what the original writers had in mind, especially if it seems clear that the persons preparing a text do not have an adequate grasp of the language in which they are writing.

3.   Pay close attention to stylistic features of a source text since these so often reveal the subtle associative (connotative) values being communicated by the writer.

4.   Translate a text only after having clearly understood its designative and associative meanings. This makes translating essentially a process of writing, in which the selection and arrangement of words is done more or less automatically.

5.   Improve the style of a translation by reading it over out-loud (even several times for some texts). Ears are much more sensitive to stylistic features than eyes, since human beings have been hearing languages for hundreds of thousands of years, but have been reading them for only a few thousand.

6.   Try to translate texts in which you have adequate background knowledge or keen interest. Nevertheless, extending the range of competence can be an interesting and personally rewarding challenge.

7.   Since translating is essentially an interlingual skill, competence increases rapidly with practice, especially if there are sources of help in dealing with special problems, for example, teachers in schools of translation, directors of agencies responsible for translation services, local societies of translators who often meet on a monthly basis to discuss common problems, and personal friends who are sensitive to problems of verbal communication.

8.   If possible, become an in-house translator of an organization in which there are different teams of translators working in different sets of languages, for example, German-Arabic, English-Chinese, and French-Russian and in different areas of technical specialization, for example, computer technology, merchandising, industrialization, law, and medicine. Such programs provide unparalleled opportunities to learn.

9.   Gradually formulate your own set of principles and procedures of translating and share these insights with others

b.   Teaching translation

1.   Have plenty of personal experience in translating so that advice and help to students will be genuine and realistic. Never try to teach a skill in which you yourself are not competent.

2.   Go over assigned texts with students and show them how to spot problems and anticipate solutions. Psychologically this is a great advantage for teachers, since it shows students that teachers really want to be helpful rather than merely judgmental.

3.   Texts assigned for translation by students should be about recent events or ideas and should be long enough for students to find most of the answers from the contexts.

4.   Teach students how to correct badly written texts as a kind of intralingual type of translating. Professional translators are constantly required to correct poorly written texts, and students need to learn how to treat such problems by dealing realistically with what they must frequently do professionally.

5.   Spend at least half of each translation session pointing out creative solutions made by students. Unfortunately, too many teachers spend entire class hours finding fault with what students have done. Such a procedure is both frustrating and largely ineffective, because people do not like to remember their mistakes but will remember their successes very positively.

6.   From time to time encourage students to work together in groups of three or four on a joint translation. Talking about the meaning of a text is an excellent approach to seeing multiple possibilities of meaning.

7.   Distinguish clearly between traditional principles and actual practice of translating by studying translations made by professional translators in terms of (1) differences in form and content, (2) evident reasons for such differences, and (3) the validity of the differences in terms of effective communication.

8.   Teach students how to analyze and grade each other's translations. Students usually pay much more attention to the judgments of school mates than to teachers, and different judgments can form the basis for realistic evaluation of principles.

9.   Undertake commercial translating. Most people learn much more from the real world than from the academic world. Money is much more convincing than grades.

CHAPTER 7

Three major types of translation theories

As yet there is no one generally accepted theory of translation in the technical sense of "a coherent set of general propositions used as principles to explain a class of phenomena," but there are several theories in the broad sense of "a set of principles that are helpful in understanding the nature of translating or in establishing criteria for evaluating a particular translated text." In general, however, these principles are stated in terms of how to produce an acceptable translation.

The lack of a fully acceptable theory of translation should not come as a surprise, because translating is essentially a very complex phenomenon, and insights concerning this interlingual activity are derived from several different disciplines, for example, linguistics, sociolinguistics, psychology, sociology, cultural anthropology, communication theory, literary criticism, aesthetics, and sociosemiotics. The fact that there is no generally accepted theory for any one of these behavioral disciplines should be a sufficient reason for people to realize that there is nothing basically inadequate about translating simply because those who translate cannot always explain by means of some comprehensive theory precisely why they do what they do.

The various sets of principles and rules about translating can be helpfully discussed in terms of historical developments, which Snell-Hornby (1988) has done very succinctly and effectively, or these principles may be discussed in terms of various disciplines that have significantly influenced the ways in which translators and interpreters have proceeded to do their work. The formulation of theories of translation has taken place primarily in the Western world and in China, where an ancient tradition of faithfulness, smoothness, and elegance was recognized as additive, not competitive.

The ancient Romans discussed at length the principles of translation embodied in the translation of Greek literature into Latin, and during the Middle Ages a great deal of translating took place in the Arab world where the ancient Latin and Greek manuscripts were translating into Arabic, many of which were in turn translated into Latin for the sake of people living in Western Europe during the Renaissance.

There are, however, certain difficulties involved in trying to discuss translation theories on a strictly historical basis. In many instances the differences
about principles of translation only reflect changing fashions about literature,
and in some instances heated arguments about how to translate seem to reflect
little more than personal prejudices and literary rivalries.

Too often the differences in theories of translation depend on extreme
positions, for example, the contention by Ortega y Gasset (1937) and Croce
(1955) that translation is really impossible. Mounin (1963) has shown how
marginal such discussions have been, and Güttinger (1963) has remarked
about how inconsistent such authors have been in wanting to have their writings translated.

Because the Bible or at least portions of it, have been translated for a longer
period of time and into more languages (2,233 as of the beginning of the year
2000), it is not strange that some of the conflicts about principles of translation
have focused on how one can legitimately translate a book that is regarded as
divinely inspired. The answer to this problem in the Arab world was to decide
that the Koran should not be translated, and as a result most translations of the
Koran have been done by non-Muslims. In Christianity, however, translating
flourished in the first few centuries (including Latin, Coptic, Syriac, Ethiopic,
Armenian, Old Church Slavonic, Gothic, and Georgian) and again during the
Reformation, but the arguments about literal or free translations reflected theological presuppositions more than linguistic concerns.

Jerome was in serious trouble for having rendered the Bible into ordinary
Latin (the Biblia Vulgata), and Luther had to defend his views of translating
into the every-day language of the German people. But in many respects his
views about translating had a major influence on freeing local languages in
Europe from the heavy hand of ecclesiastical Latin. Campbell (1789) defined
and illustrated a number of basic principles of translation in an introduction to
his own English translation of the Four Gospels, and these principles were
apparently expropriated by Tytler (1790) in a volume that is still cited as having
made a major contribution to the theory of translating.

Despite several important recent contributions to the principles of translation by those concerned with Bible translating, the actual practice of such translating has often been far less innovative and creative than the translations of the
Greek and Latin Classics in the Loeb series because over-riding theological concerns often prevented more creative and meaningful sets of correspondences.

A more useful approach to the study of the diversity of translation theories
is to group together variously related theories on the basis of the disciplines

that have served as the basic points of reference for some of the primary insights: 1. philology, although often spoken of as "literary criticism" or "literary analysis," 2. linguistics, and especially sociolinguistics (language used in communication), and 3. semiotics, particularly socio-semiotics, the study of sign systems used in human communication. This order of disciplines reflects a somewhat historical development, but each of these orientations in translating is endorsed and favored by a number of present-day scholars. At the same time it is important to recognize some of the important contributions being made to translation by other related disciplines, for example, psychology, information theory, informatics, and sociology.

There are, however, two fundamental problems in practically all approaches to theories of translating: (1) the tendency for advocates of a particular theory to build their theory on a specific discipline and often on its applicability to a single literary genre or type of discourse and (2) the primary or exclusive concern for designative (denotative) rather than associative (connotative) meanings. This is particularly true of those theories of translation that depend on some form of propositional logic to provide the categories for establishing equivalence, degrees of similarity, and acceptability.

7.1   Theories based on philological insights

Philology, the study and evaluation of written texts, including their authenticity, form, meaning, and cultural influence, has for more than 2000 years been the primary basis for discussing translation theories and practice. In general such texts have been literary productions because they seemed to be the only texts that warranted being translated into other languages.

In the Classical Roman world Cicero, Horace, Catullus, and Quintilian discussed primarily the issues of literal vs. free translating. Was a translator justified in rendering the sense of a passage at the expense of the formal features of word order and grammatical constructions? Also, should a choice metaphor be sacrificed for the sake of making sense of a passage? For the most part, Roman writers opted for freedom in translating, but the practice of translating and concern for principles of effective interlingual communication largely died out during the early Middle Ages.

With the intellectual explosion of the Renaissance *Les Belles Infideles* "the beautiful unfaithful ones" dominated the new trend in translating the Classics into the vernacular languages of Europe. And although Cowley's translation of

Pindar's Odes (1656) was by no means an extreme example of freedom in translating, Cowley was strongly criticized by Dryden (1680), who proposed a theory of translating based on three major types: metaphrase, paraphrase, and imitation. By metaphrase Dryden meant a literal, word-for-word rendering of a text, and by imitation he meant radical departures, including additions and reinterpretations. Accordingly, paraphrase was designed to represent the logical compromise between rigid word-for-word renderings and unlimited departures from an original.

In this triple approach to problems of translating literary texts, Dryden was supported by Pope (1715), but more than a century later Matthew Arnold (1862) reacted against Dryden's position and insisted on preserving the form of an original, even though the spirit and the meaning of the text were both likely to suffer. In order to illustrate the significance of his theory, Arnold translated the *Iliad* and the *Odessey* into English hexameters. Because such attempts at literal translating proved largely unacceptable, some philologists insisted that translating is simply impossible. Nevertheless, the position of Arnold, as well as the support of a number of theologians, resulted in the translation of the Revised Version of the Bible (1885), to be followed by the American Standard Version of 1901, that largely dominated Bible translating in major languages for more than fifty years.

Beginning with the twentieth century, philology experienced an infusion of new life through the recognition of insights to be gained from linguistics, especially from Russian structuralists, the Prague school, British functionalism, and anthropological linguistics in the United States. The focus of philology shifted from formal features of particular literary texts to the role of language as a code, a system for communication, and an integral part of culture. This new orientation as it relates directly to translation is well illustrated in the volumes on translation by Brower (1959), Steiner (1975) and Fowler (1977).

Perhaps the most important contribution of linguistics to philology has been in the area of text linguistics, the study of how texts are organized formally and thematically into a number of distinct types, often called "genres," for example, narratives, conversations, discourses, arguments, jokes, riddles, genealogies, sermons, lectures and lyric poetry. Some of the principal contributions to text linguistics have come from such scholars as Jakobson (1960), Halliday (1970), van Dijk (1975) and Beaugrande and Dressler (1981).

In the twentieth century philology has also been influenced by a number of French existentialist semioticians, especially Lévi Strauss (1951), Greimas (1966), Barthes (1966), and Derrida (1981). The result of this contribution to philology has been the acceptance by many persons of the separation of a text from the context out of which it has developed. Every literary text is thought to have a life its own (a kind of autonomous existence) and its interpretation need not be related to the setting out of which it arose. This approach means that interpretation depends totally upon what the reader of such a text reads into it. This orientation has resulted in some extreme views about translating, but semioticians such as Pierce, Jakobson, Eco, and Sebeok insist that a legitimate interpretation of a text cannot take place apart from the total setting of both language and culture.

7.2 Theories based on linguistic insights

Several scholars have approached the issues of translating from the viewpoints of linguistic differences between source and target texts. Some of the more important contributions include Vinay and Darbelnet's comparative analysis of French and English as a basis for a method of translating (1958), Catford's volume, *A Linguistic Theory of Translating* (1965), Toury's book *In Search of a Theory of Translation* (1980), Larson's textbook *Meaning-based Translation* (1984), and Malone's transformational-generative approach *The Science of Linguistics in the Art of Translation* (1988).

As in the case of the philological orientation to translating, linguistic theories have also been influenced and enriched by a number of developments, including cultural anthropology, philosophical approaches to semantics, information and communication theories, computational linguistics, machine translation, artificial intelligence, psycholinguistics, and sociolinguistics.

A major set of insights for translating have been derived from the study of lexical semantics by linguists involved in cultural anthropology, for example, Goodnough's work on Trukese semantic categories (1951), Lounsbury's analysis of the Pawnee kinship system (1956), the description of key semantic domains in Hopi by C. F. and F. M. Voegelin (1957), and Conklin's work in botanical taxonomies (1962). Many of these insights have been summarized and enlarge by Weinreich (1966) and Lehrer (1974). The cultural dimension in translating forms a major component in publications by Nida (1964, 1975), Nida and Taber (1969), and Snell-Hornby (1988), who entitles one chapter "Translation as a Cross-cultural Event."

Philosophers interested in their distinctive types of linguistic analysis have made primary use of various forms of propositional logic to define meanings on the basis of certain distinctive distributions. Katz and Fodor (1963) attempted to construct a semantic theory based on binary sets of distinctive features in order to treat semantics as essentially a projection of transformational-generative grammar. Bolinger (1965), however, showed how impossible this is in view of the fuzzy boundaries of meaning and the overlapping domains.

Snell-Hornby (1988) has effectively described how a number of translation theorists in Germany pushed the idea of equivalence to the point of insisting that semantic differences can and should be rigorously distinguished. In fact they went so far as to insist that true translating can only apply to nonliterary or nonfigurative texts, since they considered literary texts as structurally marginal uses of language. Fortunately, Newmark (1981) has never hesitated to say bluntly what many others have thought, namely, that when a theory becomes so arbitrary or restricted as to exclude some of the most creative and meaning-ful aspects of language, it is essentially useless.

Information theory, as formulated primarily by Wiener (1948, 1954) and Shannon and Weaver (1949) has had a very useful role in helping translators recognize the functions of redundancy. Communication theory, which is an enlargement of information theory, has helped translators see the importance of all the many factors that enter into interlingual communication: source, tar-get, transmission, noise (physical and psychological), setting, and feedback (immediate and anticipatory). Computational linguistics is especially reward-ing as it clarifies and systematizes lexical and syntactic properties of language.

Communication theory has had considerable influence on the work of Kade (1968) and Neubert (1968), and especially on the insightful studies of Reiss (1972, 1976), whose breadth of approach has been unusually effective.

Research in machine translating has also helped translators appreciate more fully the striking differences between the routine correspondences between texts and those that require creative innovation. In Wilss' volume *The Science of Translation* (1982) communication theory and machine translation figure prominently.

The linguistic orientation in translating has been especially enlarged by work in sociolinguistics, in which the emphasis is not on language as a struc-ture but on the role of language as used by speakers and writers. Sociolinguistics has called attention to the function of levels and registers in language, linguistic dialects, the roles of power and solidarity in language usage and in the systematic character of what some linguists in the past have treated as mere accidental variation. For translators the research of Labov (1966), Hymes (1974) and Lakoff and Johnson (1980) are particularly significant.

7.3 Theories based on sociosemiotics

The most pervasive and crucial contribution to an understanding of translation is to be found in sociosemiotics, the discipline that treats all the systems of signs used by human societies. The great advantage of semiotics over other approaches to interlingual communication is that it deals with all types of codes and signs. No holistic approach to translating can exclude semiotics as a fundamental discipline in encoding and decoding signs.

Semiotics is as old as the writings of Plato and Aristotle, but its present-day formulations depend in large measure on the unusual insights of Peirce (1934), the systematization of these in Eco (1979), and the practical implications of these in Sebeok (1976, 1986).

One distinct advantage of a semiotic approach to meaning is the equal attention that must be given to designative and associative meanings, because signs of all types must be understood in terms of all the other verbal signs within a text or in related texts. This focus has been particularly significant in de Beaugrande's treatments of poetic translating (1978) and in his article on schemas for literary communication (1987). Paul Friedrich has also provided important insights in his volume *The Language Parallax: Linguistic Relativism and Poetic Indeterminacy* (1986), which effectively illustrates the indeterminacy of ordinary speech and of poetic language. As an anthropologist, linguist, and poet, Friedrich is in an unusually strategic position to deal with linguistic relativism and poetic indeterminacy, with which the professional translator must wrestle each day. The continuum of order to chaos is the ultimate challenge to communication.

For an increasing number of sociologists, for example, Geertz, Sperber, and Mary Douglas, knowledge is essentially a semiotic of culture, and life is a semiotic experience, whether on the level of DNA and RNA or on the level of awe in watching a majestic aurora borealis. Because translators are constantly required to communicate knowledge and experience by means of symbols that involve varying degrees of distortion, they may find Hofstadter's concept of isomorphs helpful in dealing with problems of information preserving and information altering symbols.

As noted in Chapter 2, Wittgenstein's view of language use as essentially a game in which the parties negotiate for personal or collective advantage may provide important insight about ways of avoiding dull compromises and of finding fresh ways to express equivalences. Game theory seems to be a useful concept for translators, because language both reveals and hides, because there are always sociosemiotic factors that involved various degrees of parallax. Game theory highlights the sociological functions of language in establishing and maintaining a person's status and roles in society. This means saying the right thing at the right time to the right persons in order to maximize power and solidarity.

Game theory seems to be especially applicable to some types of literature and especially to detective stories, in which the author and readers play a constant game in trying to reveal and at the same time to hide the identity of the perpetrator of a crime. In a novel the author reveals just enough to increase constantly the reader's interest until the climax of the story is reached, at which time crucial decisions and actions resolve the crisis and a new steady state results. In good expository writing an author always tries to anticipate objections from readers and in this way negotiates for a significant advantage, while lively conversations are also an excellent example of negotiating for effective presentation and acceptance of a particular set of ideas.

Undoubtedly, one of the most effective means of learning how to translate involves a close study of what expert translators have done. A few hours of detailed investigation of the following translations and underlying texts can do a great deal to open new vistas to the nature and practice of translating: the dramas of Aristophanes by B. B. Rogers in the Loeb Classical Library, *One Hundred Years of Solitude* by Gabriel Garcia Marquez and translated by Gregory Rabassa (Avon Books), *The Name of the Rose*, by Umberto Eco and translated by William Weaver (Warner Books), *Night Flight* by Antoine de Saint-Expery translated by Stuart Gilbert, and anyone of a series of articles in German published in *Dimensions* and translated by A. Leslie Willson.

Translators will also find fascinating insights about translating in the journal *Translation Review*, published by the University of Texas at Dallas. Each issue highlights the experience of some outstanding translator who shares, usually in the form of an interview, his or her philosophy of language and important principles of translation. This hands-on approach to the successes and failures in translating is extremely helpful, because theories are always chasing practice in order to explain what has already been discovered.

Bibliography

Arnold, Matthew (1862), *On Translating Homer*. London: Longman, Green.

Baker, Mona (1992), *In Other Words*, London and New York: Routledge.

Baron, Naomi S. (1979), Functional range in speech, writing, and sign: An integrative Analysis. *Ars Semeiotica* 2:79–102. , (1981), *Speech, writing, and sign: A functional view of linguistic representation*, Bloomington: Indiana University Press.

Barthes, Roland (1966), *Critique et Vérité*. Paris: Editions Du Seuil.

Beaugrande, Robert de (1978), *Factors in a theory of poetic translating*, Assen: Van Gorcam.

Beaugrande, Robert de (1987), Schemas for literary communication. In *Literary discourse. Aspects of cognitive and social psychological approaches*, ed. by L. Halasz, 49–99. Berlin: De Gruyter.

Beaugrande, Robert de, and Wolfgang U. Dressler (1981), *Introduction to Text Linguistics*, London and New York: Longman.

Bender, John, and David E. Wellbery (1990), Rhetoricality: On the modernist return of rhetoric. In *The ends of rhetoric: History, theory, practice*, ed. by John Bender and David E. Wellbery, 3–39. Stanford, CA: Stanford University Press.

Berger, Peter L., and Thomas Luckmann (1967), *The social construction of reality: a treatise in the sociology of knowledge*. Garden City: Doubleday; New York: Anchor.

Beeby Lonsdale, Allison (1948), *Teaching Translation from Spanish to English: Worlds beyond Words*. Ottawa: University of Ottawa Press.

Bierwisch, Manfred (1980), Formal and Lexical semantics. *Linguistische Berichte* 80: 3- 17.

Bloch, Bernard, and Geoerge L. Trager (1942), *Outline of linguistic analysis*. Washington, DC: Linguistic Society of America.

Bloomfield, Leonard (1933), *Language*. New York: Holt.

Boas, Franz (1940), *Race, language, culture*. New York: Macmillan.

Bolinger, Dwight (1965), The atomization of meaning, *Language* 41 555–573.

Bolinger, Dwight (1972), *Degree words*. The Hague: Mouton.

Bolinger, Dwight (1977) *Meaning and Form*, London and New York: Longman.

Brower, Reuben A., ed. (1959) *On Translation*. Cambridge, MA: Harvard University Press

Campbell, George (1789), *The Four Gospels*. London: Strahan and Cadell.

Catford, J. C. (1965), *A linguistic theory of translation*. London: Oxford University Press.

Chafe, Wallace L. (1970), *Meaning and the structure of language*. Chicago: University of Chicago Press.

Chomsky, Noam (1965) *A linguistic theory of translation*. Cambridge, MA: MIT Press.

Chomsky, Noam (1972) *Studies on semantics in generative grammar*. The Hague: Mouton

Chomsky, Noam (1974) *Reflections on language*. New York: Pantheon.

Chomsky, Noam (1986) *Barriers*. Cambridge, MA: MIT Press.

Coleman, Linda and Paul Kay (1981), Prototype semantics: The English word *lie*. *Language* 57: 26–44.

Conklin, Harold D. (1962), Lexicographical treatment of folk taxonomies, *International Journal of American Linguistics* 28: 119–141.

Cowley, Abraham (1656), *Preface to "Pindarique odes" Poems*. London: Humphrey Moseley.

Croce, Benedetto (1902, 1955), *Filosofia, poesia, storia: Pagine tratte da tutte le opere a cara dell' autore*. Milano: Ricciardi.

Croitoru, Elena (1996), *Interpretation and Translation*. Galati, Rumania: Editura Porto Franco.

Cruse, D. A. (1986), *Lexical semantics*. Cambridge and New York: Cambridge University Press.

Derrida, Jacques (1981), *Positions*. Chicago: University of Chicago Press.

Dryden, John (1680), *Preface to Ovid's epistles*. London: Jacob Tonson.

Damasio, Antonio R. (1994), *Descartes' Error: Emotion, Reason, and the Human Brain*. New York: Avon Books.

Eco, Umberto (1979), *A theory of semiotics*. Advances in Semiotics. Bloomington: Indiana University Press.

Fillmore, Charles J. (1965), Entailment rules in semantic theory. Project on Linguistic Analysis, Report no. 10, 6082. Columbus: Ohio State University Research Foundation.

Fillmore, Charles J. (1967), The case for case. *Proceedings of the 1967 Texas conference on language universals*, ed. by E. Bach and R. Harms, 1–88. New York: Holt Rinehart and Winston.

Firth, John Rupert (1957), *Papers in Linguistics*. Oxford: Oxford University Press.

Fowler, Roger (1957), *Linguistics and the novel*. London and New York: Methuen.

Friedrich, Paul (1977), *Language, context, and the imagination*. Stanford, CA: Stanford University Press.

Friedrich, Paul (1986), *The language parallax: Linguistic relativism and poetic indeterminacy*. Austin: University of Texas Press.

Fromkin, Victoria, and Robert Rodman (1978), *An introduction to language, 2nd edition*. New York: Holt, Ricehart and Winston.

Gile, Daniel (1995), *Basic Concepts and Models for Interpreter and Translator Training*. Amsterdam and Philadelphia: John Benjamins Publishing Company.

Goodenough, Ward H. (1951), *Property, kin, and community on Truk*. New Haven: Yale University Press.

Greimas, A. J. (1966), *Semantique Structurale*. Paris: Librairie Larouse.

Grice, H. P. (1968), Utterer's meaning, sentence-meaning, and word-meaning, *Foundations of Language* 4:225–242.

Guattari, Felix (1981), Interpretance and significance. *Semiotica* supp. 119–125.

Gumperz, John Joseph (1982) *Language and social identity*. Cambridge and New York: Cambridge University Press.

Güttinger, Fritz (1963), Zielsprache: Theorie und Technik des Übersetzens. Zürich: Manasse.

Gutt, Ernst-August (1991), *Translation and Relevance*. Oxford and Cambridge: Basil Blackwell Ltd.

Haiman, John (1980),The iconicity of grammar. *Language* 56: 515–540.

Halliday, M. A. K. (1970), Descriptive linguistics in literary studies, In *Linguistics and literary style*, ed. By Donald C. Freeman, 57–72. New York: Holt Rinehart and Winston.

Halliday, M. A. K. (1978), *Language and social semiotic: The social interpretation of language and meaning*. Baltimore, MD: University Park Press; London: Edward Arnold Publishers.

Halliday, M. A. K. and Ruqaiya Hasan (1976), *Cohesion in English*. London: Longman.

Harris, Zellig S. (1957), Co-occurrence and transformation in linguistic structure. *Language* 33:283–340

Hatim, Basil and Ian Mason (1990), *Discourse and the Translator*. Harlow (Essex): Longman group UK, Limited.

Hockett, Charles F. (1958), *A course in modern linguistics*. New York: Macmillan.

Hofstadter, Douglas R. (1980), *Goedel, Escher, Bach; An eternal golden braid*. New York: Random House.

Hoijer, Harry (1951), Cultural implications of some Navaho linguistic categories, *Language* 27:111–120.

Hymes, Dell (1974), *Foundations in sociolinguistics: An ethnographic approach*. Philadelphia: University of Pennsylvania Press.

Ikegami, Yoshihiko (1967), Structural semantics: A survey and problems, *Linguistics* 33:46–67.

Jakobson, Roman (1960), Linguistics and poetics, In *Style in language*, ed. by Thomas A. Sebeok, 350–377. Cambridge, MA: Technology Press.

Jakobson, Roman (1963), Implications of language universals for linguistics, In *Universals of language*, ed. By J. H. Greenberg, 208–219. Cambridge, MA: MIT Press.

Jakobson, Roman (1970), *Main trends in the science of language*. New York: Harper and Row.

Jakobson, Roman (1972), `Verbal Communication' *Scientific American*, 227, pp. 72–81.

Jakobson, Roman (1960), *Framework of language*. Ann Arbor: Michigan Slavic Publications.

Joos, Martin (1958), Semology: A Linguistic Theory of Meaning, *Studies in Linguistics* 13, 53–70

Joos, Martin (1962), The Five Clocks, *International Journal of Linguistics* 28, No. 2, Part V, Publication 22 of the Indiana University Research Center in Anthropology, Folklore, and Linguistics.

Joos, Martin (1972), Semantic axiom number one, *Language* 48: 257–265.

Kade, Otto (1968),Kommunikationswissenschaftliche Probleme der Ubersetzung, In *Grundfragen der Ubersetzungswissenschaft*, ed. By A. Neubert. Beihefte zur Zeitschrift Fremdsprachen 2: 3–20.

Katz, Jerrold J., and Jerry Fodor (1963), The structure of a semantic theory, *Language* 39:170–210.

Komissarov, Vilen (1987), The semantic and the cognitive in the text: A problem of equivalence. *META* 32: 416–419.

Krampen, Martin (1979), Profusion of signs without confusion. *Ars Semeiotica* 2:327- 359.

Labov, William (1966), *The social stratification of English in New York City*. Washington D. C.: Center for Applied Linguistics.

Labov, William (1972), *Language in the inner city*. Philadelphia: University of Pennsylvania Press.

Labov, William (1978), Denotational structure, In *Papers from the parasession on the lexicon*, ed. by Donna Farkas, 220–260. Chicago: Chicago Linguistic Society.

Ladmiral, J-R (1979), *Traduire: Théorèmes pour la traduction*. Paris: Payot.

Lakoff, George, and Mark Johnson (1980), *Metaphors we live by*. Chicago: University of Chicago Press.

Lamb, Sydney M. (1966), *Outline of stratificational grammar*. Washington, D. C.: Georgetown University Press.

Larson, Mildred L. (1984), *Meaning-based translation: A guide to cross-language equivalence*. Lanham, MD: University Press of America.

Laszlo, Antal (1963), Interpretation and transformation. *Linguistics* 2:16–25.

Leech, Geoffrey N. (1970) *Towards a semantic description of English*. Bloomington: Indiana University Press.

Lehrer, Adrienne (1974) *Semantic fields and lexical structure*. Amsterdam: North- Holland Publishing Company.

Lévi-Srauss, Claude (1951), Language and the analysis of social laws, *American Anthropologist* 53:155–163,

Levinson, S. C. (1983), *Pragmatics*. Cambridge: Cambridge University Press.

Lisse, Peter de Ridder, and Thomas A. Sebeok (1986), *Encyclopedic dictionary of semiotics*- Berlin: Mouton de Gruyter.

Lópes Guix, Juan Gabriel and Jacqueline Minett Wilkinson (1997), *Manual de Traducción*. Barcelona: Editorial Gedisa.

Lounsbury, Floyd G. (1955), The varieties of meaning. In Monograph Series No. 8, 158–164. Washington, D.C.:Georgetown University Institute of Language and Linguistics.

Lounsbury, Floyd G. (1956), A semantic analysis of the Pawnee kinship usage. *Language* 32:158- 194.

Louw, Johannes P., and Eugene A. Nida (1988,1989), *Greek-English lexicon of the New Testament based on semantic domains*. New York: United Bible Societies.

Lyons, John (1977), *Semantics*. Cambridge: Cambridge University Press.

Makkai, Adam (1972), *Idiom structure in English*. The Hague: Mouton.

Malinowski, Bronislaw (1922), *Argonauts of the western Pacific*. London: Routledge.

Malone, Joseph L. (1988), *The science of linguistics in the art of translation*. Albany: State University of New York Press.

McCawley, James D. (1988), *The syntactic phenomena of English*.(2 volumes). Chicago and London: University of Chicago Press.

Merrell, Floyd (1979) Some signs that preceded their times: or are we really ready for Peirce? *Ars Semeiotica* 2:149.172.

Merrell, Floyd (1980), Of metaphor and metonymy, *Semiotica* 31:249–307.

Merrell, Floyd (1984), Deconstruction meets a mathematician: metasemiotic inquiry. *Semiotics* 2:125–152.

Miller, George A. (1978), Semantic relations among words, in *Linguistic theory and psychological reality*, ed. by Morris Halle, Joan Bresnan, and George A. Miller, 60–118. Cambridge MA and London: MIT Press.

Miller, George A. and P. N. Johnson-Laird (1976), *Language and group perception*. Cambridge, MA: Harvard University Press; Cambridge: Cambridge University Press.

Moravscik, J. M. E. (1972), Review of *Towards a semantic description of English* by Geoffrey N. Leech (Bloomington: Indiana University Press, 1970). *Language* 48:445–454.

Morris, Charles W. (1938), Foundations of a theory of signs. In *International encyclopedia of unified science* vol. 2.63–75. Chicago:University of Chicago Press.

Morris, Charles W. (1964), *Signification and significance.* Cambridge: MIT Press.

Mounin, Georges (1963), *Les problèmes théoriques de la tradicion.* Paris: Gallimard.

Mounin, Georges (1972), *Clefs pour la sémantique.* Paris: Editions Seghers.

Murray, Stephen O., and Robert C. Poolman, Jr. (1984), Socially structuring prototype semantics. *Forum Linguisticum* 8:95–102.

Nauta, Doede, Jr. (1972), *The meaning of information.* The Hague: Mouton.

Neubert, Albrecht (1968), Pragmatische Aspekte der Ubersetzung, in *Grundfragen de Ubersetzungswissenschaft,* ed. by A. Neubert, Beihefte zur Zeitschrift Fremdsprachen 2:21–33.

Newmark, Peter (1981), *Approaches to translation.* Oxford: Pergamon.

Nida, Eugene A. (1964), *Toward a Science of Translating,* Leiden: E. J. Brill.

Nida, Eugene A. (1975), *Componential Analysis of Meaning.* The Hague: Mouton.

Nida, Eugene A. (1975), *Exploring semantic structures.* Munich: Wilhelm Fink.

Nida, Eugene A. and Charles R. Taber (1969), *The theory and practice of translation.* Leiden: Brill.

Ortega y Gasset, Jose. (1937), *Miseria y esplendor de la traducción,* Obras Completas, 5: 427–448.

Osgood, Charles E., George J. Suci, and Percy H. Tannenbaum (1957), *The measurement of meaning.* Urbana: University of Illinois Press.

Osgood, Charles E., William H. May and Murray S. Miron (1975), *Cross-cultural universals of affective meaning.* Urbana: University of Illinois Press.

Palmer, F. R. (1976) *Semantics: A new outline.* Cambridge: Cambridge University Press.

Partee, Barabara H. (1977), Possible Worlds semantics and linguistic theory. *The Monist* 60: 303–326.

Pierce, Charles (1934), *Collected papers.* Cambridge, MA: Harvard University Press.

Percival, W. Keith (1981), The Saussurean paradigm: Fact or fantasy? *Semiotica* 36:33- 49.

Pergnier, Maurice (1993), *Les Fondements Sociolinguistiques de la Traduction,* Lille: P r e s s e s Universitaires de Lille.

Pike, Kenneth L. (1954–55), *Language in relation to a unified theory of the structure of human behavior.* Glendale, CA: Summer Institute of Linguistics.

Propp, V. (1958), *Morphology of the folktale.* Folklore and Linguistics. Bloomington: Indiana University Research Center in Anthropology.

Quine, Willard Van Orman (1960), *Word and object.* Cambridge, MA: MIT Press, and New York: Wiley.

Reiss, Katharina (1971), *Texttyp und Ubersetzungsmethode.* Kronberg: Scriptor

Rey-Dehove, J., ed. (1973), *Recherches sur les systèmes signifiants.* The Hague: Mouton.

Richards, I. A. (1953), Toward a theory of translating, in *Studies in Chinese Thought,* ed. by Arthur f. Wright, 247–262. American Anthropological Association, vol. 55, memoir 75. Chicago: Chicago University Press.

Ricoeur, Paul (1969), *Le conflit des interprétations: essais d'herméneutique.* Paris: Editions de Seuil.

Robinson, Douglas (1985), C. S. Peirce and dialogic pragmatism. *Kodikas/Code* 8:179- 194.

Sadock, Jerrold M. (1986), The position of vagueness among insecurities of language. *Quaderni de Semantica* 14:267–276.

Sagan, Carl (1980), *Cosmos*, New York: Random House.

Sapir, Edward (1939). *Language: An introduction to the study of speech.* New York: Harcourt, Brace.

Saussure, Ferdinand de (1959), *Course in general linguistics.* New York: Philosophical Library.

Searle, John R. (1969), *Speech acts: An essay in the philosophy of language.* Cambridge: Cambridge University Press.

Sebeok, Thomas A. (1976), *Contributions to the doctrine of signs.* Bloomington, IN: Research Center for Language and Semiotic Studies.

Sebeok, Thomas A. and Jean Sebeok-Umiker (1079), You know my method: A juxtaposition of Charles S. Peirce and Sherlock Holmes. *Semiotica*: 26:203–250.

Shannon, Claude L., and Warren Weaver (1949), *The mathematical theory of communication.* Urbana: University of Illinois Press.

Snell-Hornby, Mary (1988), *Translation Studies, an Integrated Approach,* Amsterdam and Philadelphia: John Benjamins Publishing Company.

Sperber, Dan (1975), *Rethinking symbolism.* Cambridge Studies and Papers in Social Anthropology. Cambridge: Cambridge University Press.

Steinberg, D. D., and L. A. Jacobovitz, eds. (1971), *Semantics: An interdisciplinary reader in philosophy, linguistics, and psychology.* Cambridge: Cambridge University Press.

Steiner, George (1975), *After Babel: Aspects of language and translation.* London: Oxford University Press.

Sturtevant, William C. (1964), Studies in ethnoscience. *American Anthropologist* 66:99–103.

Toury, Gideon (1989), *In search of a theory of translation.* Tel Aviv: Porter Institute for Poetics and Semiotics, Tel Aviv University.

Traugott, Elizabeth Closs (1978), On the expression of spatio-temporal relations in language. In *Universals of human language,* ed. by Joseph H. Greenberg, 369- 400. Stanford, CA: Stanford University Press.

Trubetskoy, Nikolai Sergieevich (1939), *Principes de phonologie.* Paris: Klinksieck.

Umiker-Sebeok, Jean (1979), Nature's way? Visual images of childhood in American culture. *Semiotica* 27:173–220.

Van Dijk, Teun A. (1975), Formal semantics of metaphorical discourse. *Poetics* 4: 173- 198.

Vázquez-Ayora, Gerardo (1977), *Introducción a la Traductología.* Washington, D. C.: Georgetown University Press.

Vinay, J.-P., and J. Darbelnet (1958), *Stylistique comparée du francais et de anglais: Méthod de traduction.* Paris: Didier; Montreal: Beauchemin.

Voegelin, C. F. (1948), Distinctive features and meaning equivalence. *Language* 24:132- 135.
, and Florence M. Voegelin (1957), Hopi domains, a lexical approach to the problem of selection. *International Journal of American Linguistics,* Memoir no. 14.

Waard, Jan de, and Eugene A. Nida (1986) *From one language to another.* Nashville: Thomas Nelson.

Wald, Lucia (1979), Le rapport entre signum et denotatum dans la conception d'Augustin, in *A semiotic landscape / parorama semiotique*, ed. by S. Chatman, Umberto Eco, and J. M. Klinkenberg, 569–572. The Hague: Mouton.

Weinreich, Uriel (1958), Travels in semantic space. *Word* 14:346–366. , (1963), On the semantic structure of language. In *Theoretical foundations*, vol. 3, ed. by Joseph H. Greenberg, 114–171. Cambridge, MA: MIT Press. , (1966), Explorations in semantic theory, In *Theoretical foundations*, vol. 3 of *Current trends in linguistics*, ed by Thomas A. Sebeok, 395–477. The Hague: Mouton. , (1980), *On semantics*. Philadelphia: University of Pennsylvania Press.

Wells, Rulon S. (1954), Meaning and use. *Word* 10: 235–250.

Whorf, Benjamin Lee (1973), *Language, thought and reality; Selected writings*, ed. by John B. Carroll. Cambridge, MA: MIT Press.

Wiener, Norbert (1948), *Cybernetics, or control and communication in the animal and the machine*. New York: Wiley.

Wiersbicka, Anna (1972), *Semantic primitives*. Frankfurt: Athenaeum. , (1988), *The semantics of grammar*. Amsterdam and Philadelphia: John Benjamins.

Wilss, Wolfram (1982), *The science of translation: Problems and methods*. Tübingen: Gunter Narr. ,(1996), *Knowledge and Skills in Translator Behavior*. Amsterdam and Philadelphia: John Benjamins Publishing Company.

Witherspoon, Gary, (1980), Language in culture and culture in language. *International Journal of American Linguistics* 46: 1–13.

Wittgenstein, Ludwig (1958), *Philosophical investigations*. New York: Macmillan, Oxford: Blackwell.

Wotjak, Gerd (1971), *Untersuchungen sur Strucktur der Bedeutung*. Berlin: Max Hueber.

Yri, Kjell Magne (1998), *My father taught me how to cry, but now I have forgotten: The semantics of religious concepts with emphasis on meaning, interpretation, and translatability*, Oslo: Scandinavian University Press.

Zwicky, Arnold M. (1973), inguistics as chemistry: The substance theory of semantic primes. In *A festschrift for Morris Halle*, ed. by Stephen R. Anderson and Paul Kiparsky, 467–485. New York: Holt, Rinehart and Winston.

Index

In the BENJAMINS TRANSLATION LIBRARY the following titles have been published thus far or are scheduled for publication:

1. SAGER, Juan C: *Language Engineering and Translation: Consequences of automation,* 1994.
2. SNELL-HORNBY, Mary, Franz PÖCHHACKER and Klaus KAINDL (eds): *Translation Studies: An interdiscipline. Selected papers from the Translation Congress, Vienna, 9–12 September 1992.* 1994.
3. LAMBERT, Sylvie and Barbara MOSER-MERCER (eds): *Bridging the Gap: Empirical research on simultaneous interpretation.* 1994.
4. TOURY, Gideon: *Descriptive Translation Studies — and beyond.* 1995.
5. DOLLERUP, Cay and Annette LINDEGAARD (eds): *Teaching Translation and Interpreting 2: Insights, aims, visions. Selected papers from the Second Language International Conference, Elsinore, 4–6 June 1993.* 1994.
6. EDWARDS, Alicia Betsy: *The Practice of Court Interpreting.* 1995.
7. BEAUGRANDE, Robert de, Abdulla SHUNNAQ and Mohamed Helmy HELIEL (eds): *Language Discourse and Translation in the West and Middle East. Selected and revised papers from the conference on Language and Translation, Irbid, Jordan 1992.* 1994.
8. GILE, Daniel: *Basic Concepts and Models for Interpreter and Translator Training.* 1995.
9. REY, Alain: *Essays on Terminology.* 1995.
10. KUSSMAUL, Paul: *Training the Translator.* 1995.
11. VINAY, Jean Paul and Jean DARBELNET: *Comparative Stylistics of French and English: A methodology for Translation.* 1995.
12. BERGENHOLTZ, Henning and Sven TARP: *Manual of Specialised Lexicography: The preparation of specialised dictionaries.* 1995.
13. DELISLE, Jean and Judith WOODSWORTH (eds): *Translators through History.* 1995.
14. MELBY, Alan with Terry WARNER: *The Possibility of Language. A discussion of the nature of language, with implications for human and machine translation.* 1995.
15. WILSS, Wolfram: *Knowledge and Skills in Translator Behavior.* 1996.
16. DOLLERUP, Cay and Vibeke APPEL: *Teaching Translation and Interpreting 3. New Horizons. Papers from the Third Language International Conference, Elsinore, Denmark 9–11 June 1995.* 1996.
17. POYATOS, Fernando (ed.): *Nonverbal Communication and Translation. New perspectives and challenges in literature, interpretation and the media.* 1997.
18. SOMERS, Harold (ed.): *Terminology, LSP and Translation. Studies in language engineering in honour of Juan C. Sager.* 1996.
19. CARR, Silvana E., Roda P. ROBERTS, Aideen DUFOUR and Dini STEYN (eds): *The Critical Link: Interpreters in the Community. Papers from the 1st international conference on interpreting in legal, health and social service settings, Geneva Park, Canada, 1–4 June 1995.* 1997.
20. SNELL-HORNBY, Mary, Zuzana JETTMAROVÁ and Klaus KAINDL (eds): *Translation as Intercultural Communication. Selected papers from the EST Congress – Prague 1995.* 1997.
21. BUSH, Peter and Kirsten MALMKJÆR (eds): *Rimbaud's Rainbow. Literary translation in higher education.* 1998.
22. CHESTERMAN, Andrew: *Memes of Translation. The spread of ideas in translation theory.* 1997.

23. GAMBIER, Yves, Daniel GILE and Christopher TAYLOR (eds): *Conference Interpreting: Current Trends in Research. Proceedings of the International Conference on Interpreting: What do we know and how?* 1997.
24. ORERO, Pilar and Juan C. SAGER (eds): *Translators on Translation. Giovanni Pontiero.* 1997.
25. POLLARD, David E. (ed.): *Translation and Creation. Readings of Western Literature in Early modern China, 1840–1918.* 1998.
26. TROSBORG, Anna (ed.): *Text Typology and Translation.* 1997.
27. BEYLARD-OZEROFF, Ann, Jana KRÁLOVÁ and Barbara MOSER-MERCER (eds): *Translator Strategies and Creativity. Selected Papers from the 9th International Conference on Translation and Interpreting, Prague, September 1995. In honor of Jiří Levi and Anton Popovic.* 1998.
28. SETTON, Robin: *Simultaneous Interpretation. A cognitive-pragmatic analysis.* 1999.
29. WILSS, Wolfram: *Translation and Interpreting in the 20th Century. Focus on German.* 1999.
30. DOLLERUP, Cay: *Tales and Translation. The Grimm Tales from Pan-Germanic narratives to shared international fairytales.* 1999.
31. ROBERTS, Roda P., Silvana E. CARR, Diana ABRAHAM and Aideen DUFOUR (eds): *The Critical Link 2: Interpreters in the Community. Papers from the Second International Conference on Interpreting in legal, health and social service settings, Vancouver, BC, Canada, 19–23 May 1998.* 2000.
32. BEEBY, Allison, Doris ENSINGER and Marisa PRESAS (eds): *Investigating Translation. Selected papers from the 4th International Congress on Translation, Barcelona, 1998.* 2000.
33. GILE, Daniel, Helle V. DAM, Friedel DUBSLAFF, Bodil MARTINSEN and Anne SCHJOLDAGER (eds): *Getting Started in Interpreting Research.* 2001.
34. GAMBIER, Yves and Henrik GOTTLIEB (eds): *(Multi) Media Translation. Concepts, practices, and research.* 2001.
35. In preparation.
36. SCHMID, Monika S.: *Translating the Elusive. Marked word order and subjectivity in English-German translation.* 1999.
37. TIRKKONEN-CONDIT, Sonja and Riitta JÄÄSKELÄINEN (eds): *Tapping and Mapping the Processes of Translation and Interpreting. Outlooks on empirical research.* 2000.
38. SCHÄFFNER, Christina and Beverly ADAB (eds): *Developing Translation Competence.* 2000.
39. CHESTERMAN, Andrew, Natividad GALLARDO SAN SALVADOR and Yves GAMBIER (eds): *Translation in Context. Selected papers from the EST Congress, Granada 1998.* 2000.
40. ENGLUND DIMITROVA, Birgitta and Kenneth HYLTENSTAM (eds): *Language Processing and Simultaneous Interpreting. Interdisciplinary perspectives.* 2000.
41. NIDA, Eugene A.: *Contexts in Translating.* 2002.
42. HUNG, Eva (ed.): *Teaching Translation and Interpreting 4. Building bridges.* 2002
43. GARZONE, Giuliana and Maurizio VIEZZI (eds): *Interpreting in the 21st Century. Challenges and opportunities.* n.y.p.
44. SINGERMAN, Robert: *Jewish Translation History. A bibliography of bibliographies and studies.* 2002.